WHO RULES IN YOUR LIFE?

Reflections on Personal Power

First published by O Books, 2008
O Books is an imprint of John Hunt Publishing
Ltd., The Bothy, Deershot Lodge, Park Lane,
Ropley, Hants, SO24 0BE, UK
office1@o-books.net
www.o-books.net

Distribution in:

UK and Europe
Orca Book Services
orders@orcabookservices.co.uk
Tel: 01202 665432 Fax: 01202 666219
Int. code (44)

USA and Canada
NBN
custserv@nbnbooks.com
Tel: 1 800 462 6420 Fax: 1 800 338 4550

Australia and New Zealand
Brumby Books
sales@brumbybooks.com.au
Tel: 61 3 9761 5535 Fax: 61 3 9761 7095

Far East (offices in Singapore, Thailand,
Hong Kong, Taiwan)
Pansing Distribution Pte Ltd
kemal@pansing.com
Tel: 65 6319 9939 Fax: 65 6462 5761

South Africa
Alternative Books
altbook@peterhyde.co.za
Tel: 021 555 4027 Fax: 021 447 1430

Text copyright Miriam Subirana and
Ramon Ribalta 2008

Design: Stuart Davies
Painting on the cover by Miriam Subirana.
Title: Flow

ISBN: 978 1 84694 117 1

A CIP catalogue record for this book is available
from the British Library.

Translator: Steve Cedar
Original title: ¿Quién manda en tu vida?
Reflexiones sobre la soberania personal.
By Rba-Integral, Barcelona, Spain.

Printed by Chris Fowler International
www.chrisfowler.com

O Books operates a distinctive and ethical publishing philosophy in
all areas of its business, from its global network of authors to
production and worldwide distribution.
This book is produced on FSC certified stock, within ISO14001
standards. The printer plants sufficient trees each year through
the Woodland Trust to absorb the level of emitted carbon in
its production.

WHO RULES IN YOUR LIFE?

Reflections on Personal Power

MIRIAM SUBIRANA
RAMÓN RIBALTA

BKIS

BOOKS

Winchester, UK
Washington, USA

CONTENTS

PROLOGUE

Humanity is passing through one of its most critical periods in history. To be able to face today's challenges we must be aware of all our resources and develop our inner potential.

To live in a dignified and coherent way in this increasingly competitive and aggressive society, we must maintain an emotional, mental and spiritual balance that enables us to come up with suitable and beneficial responses at all times.

If we know ourselves better and we create a space of peace and silence in our minds we will be able to understand the meaning of our existence that much better, and be able to deal with the problems, hurries, conflicts and tensions that confront us daily and which sometimes make it hard for us to enjoy life to the full.

The reflections in this book provide an understanding of human consciousness and through meditation provide a simple method of putting them into practice in our day-to-day lives.

The wisdom you will find here comes from the teachings that are given in the Brahma Kumaris World Spiritual University. On the Brahma Kumaris courses the students learn to discover themselves and are given the methodology and wisdom to reach a state of inner power and self rule.

This knowledge may be useful for you to attain a state of greater freedom and personal autonomy. In any case, to achieve results you must practice daily with commitment and concentration. You will no doubt benefit from the results of your efforts and they will help you feel that living is marvellous when you are able to once again rediscover all your inner beauty and wisdom.

INTRODUCTION

Thoughts and thought models have a big influence over our lives. Many people are not aware of the effect they have. Thinking is something we do every day throughout the whole day. In fact, we never stop thinking. Even when we sleep we continue thinking in dreams.

When you form your thoughts you produce feelings, attitudes, words and actions that make up the book or painting of your life. You are the artist and creator.

This book takes you into the wisdom that teaches you to produce the highest quality of thoughts whenever and wherever you wish. Getting out of the routine so that you are no longer influenced by the whirlwind of your thoughts and emotions, and by those created by others around you, depends on you.

As a result of the daily bombardment of information (television, telephones, work and media), we have rendered our hearts insensitive and find it hard to control the flight and speed of our thoughts and to put them into practice. All this has distanced us from our true identity, who is behind these masks and protective armour, attitudes and roles. We have come to believe that we are in fact these roles and we identify ourselves with them.

One of the aims of this book is to help you become aware of the quality of your thoughts. You can live each moment of your life knowing how to choose beneficial and quality thoughts quite consciously, and learn to protect yourself from diverse negative influences.

To improve the quality of your thoughts you must be aware of how you think, and recognise that each one of us creates our own thoughts, whether positive or useless and negative. From this you can lay the basis for real positive change in your life.

Look at your thoughts and how you feel. From here a natural desire arises to try and understand several things: why do I think and feel like this? Where do these thoughts come from? By looking into your inner self, or to put it another way, being introspective, in order to understand what creates these thoughts, you will probably come across a series of deeply-rooted habits within you.

The only way of strengthening the power you have to choose and make it effective is through an inner voyage to understand and manage how your mind works in a better way. This is what meditation is all about.

This book will guide you in being aware of the influence your thoughts have over your quality of life; being aware of the creative capacity you have to choose the kind of thoughts you want to create at any time; developing a more positive attitude towards life; and creating positive thoughts and feelings before going in to situations. It will also enable you to learn meditation as a way of channelling the energy of your mind, which will help you to widen the understanding of your spiritual identity and discover your potential abilities and powers.

Thoughts and thought patterns have a big influence in out lives. Many people do not think about the repercussion of their thoughts. When you create thoughts you generate feelings, attitudes, words, and actions, you create the picture of your life. It is up to you to break with routine in order not to be influenced by the turmoil of your thoughts.

One of the objectives of this book is to help you to be aware of the quality of your thoughts. You can live every moment of your life knowing how to choose consciously good and beneficial thoughts, and learn to protect yourself from negative influences.

In order to improve the quality of your thoughts, you have to be aware of the way you think and recognise that each one of us creates our thoughts, whether positive, wasteful or negative. To recognise this situation allows you to lay the foundations of a true positive change in your life.

- Recognise the influence that thoughts have in your life
- Be aware of your creative capacity
- Develop an attitude more positive
- Widen the understanding of your spiritual identity

- Learn about meditation as a method to channel the energy of your mind
- Develop your virtues

Positive Thinking

It is important to clarify some misconceptions regarding positive thinking, since some people think that a positive thinker always goes round with a good-natured smile on their face thinking that everything is hunky-dory. Whatever happens, they will just tell you to keep smiling. Others believe that positive thinking turns us into timid and weak people.

It is not like that though. The more we understand and experiment with our own inner qualities and powers, the stronger we become and less we depend on others. Knowing our own weaknesses can also help us to become stronger and more stable people.

Why do we want to be positive? Because being positive means being in harmony. Just as our bodies are 80 per cent water and this is the element that we most need daily, so our inner selves also need positivity, because that is what it is.

We spend our lives in search of peace, happiness, love, truth and wisdom, our most genuine qualities. What we are looking for in our lives, what we are yearning for, we already possess in our inner selves. We simply have to rediscover it.

Positive thinking is a mental attitude. It is a way of seeing life. It means doing things with assertiveness. It is a way of behaving and taking a position before events, situations and people. Life is no longer a whole series of problems and becomes a chance to learn and to grow.

CHAPTER 1

ADVANTAGES OF POSITIVE THINKING

How Do You Know if a Thought is Positive?
The thoughts that arise from your purest and most genuine soul are positive. A positive thought brings out the best in you and fills you with enthusiasm. A positive thought always has a beneficial effect, on you, society or the world, and harms no one. A positive thought about yourself boosts your self-confidence and helps you to recognize and appreciate your qualities.

Being aware of your spiritual identity, you are connecting with your true qualities, and the thoughts you create from this consciousness are positive.

What Stops You from Being Positive?
There are many reasons that make it difficult to produce and hold on to positivity in your mind and attitude. The external information we receive is mainly negative news, and our conversations are based on this news. Other causes include other people's negativity rubbing off on you; other people's criticisms influencing you; self-doubt; lacking clear objectives in life; not having recognized your qualities, virtues and values; lacking self-confidence; not believing you are a positive person; keeping the past in your mind; having a big ego; comparing yourself with others; having low self-esteem; being frustrated or irritated; and lacking flexibility or tolerance with people or situations.

Negative influences lead you to:
Create negative feelings
Lose your self-esteem
Project your failings and weaknesses onto other people
Make communication with others more difficult

Have problems sleeping soundly

Reduce your ability to choose freely (which can lead to dependencies).

The Benefits on Positive Thinking on the Mind, Body and Relationships

There are many advantages of positive thinking.

On the mind

You are more creative

You think more clearly

You strengthen your ability to concentrate on quality thoughts that in turn produce good feelings

You acquire more self-respect and respect towards others

You generate the ability of self-control and strength in difficult situations

You overcome pressures and worries more easily

You experience peace, calm, serenity and happiness.

On the body

You feel more relaxed physically

You feel more active with more energy

Your energy flows better and you feel more active

Your breathing improves, being slower and deeper

Your immunological system is strengthened and your digestive system improves

The nervous system is strengthened

Your mind is balanced and in harmony and your health improves.

On relationships

Your relationships are more harmonious

You possess greater ability to accept others with comprehension and without expectations

Your positive thoughts influence others and you share your

happiness

You attract other people with your peace and harmony

You make others approach your true self and they feel comfortable with you

You break through barriers and build solid bridges of communication and understanding

The Power of Choosing

Inner freedom is the ability we have to be the creators of our own thoughts and feelings. It is the freedom to think, experience and express who we really are, when we love and for the time we want. How can you develop the power to choose your own thoughts and feelings? What thoughts should you create that enable you to experience wellbeing and inner freedom? How can you free yourself of negative influences?

When you learn to separate yourself from the influences around you, you can discover your true self and recognise yourself as you are, and not as a reflection of what others think of you.

You can have true freedom when:

You strengthen and maintain your positive qualities in your consciousness (such as love, peace and wisdom), and you do not allow external negative influences to enter into your mind and weaken you

You accept that everyone is their own person and has their own role in life

You accept situations and deal with them or transform them (according to each case) with a positive attitude. This is possible when you learn to enter into and remain in silence and objectively observe from this space that silence helps you to create.

Thinking positively helps you to have an open mind and to be prepared to find solutions to problems, not escaping from reality but also not falling into a negative spiral because of them.

Being positive means always finding the best way possible of

responding to each situation in your life.

Positivity in Action

When you do not control your thoughts you are ruled by your emotions, by the registers recorded in your mind and your memories or by circumstances or by the environment which you are in. Your life is therefore controlled by internal and external conditionings. This reactive nature leads you to live an emotionally unstable life.

Positive thinking helps you to be the person in charge of their own life. You do not blame others for situations or problems that arise. You do not determine your behaviour as a result of the conditions or circumstances, but as a result of your own conscious choice, which may be based on carefully selected and interiorised values.

Learn to Create Healthy Habits for Maintaining a Healthy Attitude Towards Life

Accept yourself
Devote time in your life to know yourself
Assess and evaluate yourself positively
Give and receive love
Consider the past as the past
Be responsible for yourself
Appreciate the positive
Learn and develop your inner resources
Learn and develop social skills
Be yourself.

A Constructive Attitude

If we complain about the things we see and do not like and do nothing to change them, it is probably because we do not have the creativity and inner strength to provide a positive response to this situation and transform it.

When we complain about some external circumstance, it means

that in our minds we must have an image of how we think things should be, but we are not prepared to commit ourselves and do something that will change that image into reality. If we were really prepared we would not complain about what is happening outside, we would know that complaining and finger-pointing is not the best way to find a solution to situations we find ourselves in.

When we cooperate with a positive and constructive attitude to improve our immediate surroundings, it benefits both ourselves and others.

We can all choose how to respond to a specific situation, and that is where true freedom begins, which lies in the choice of how we respond to situations and aspects that are outside us.

CHAPTER 2

THE POWER AND EFFECT OF
THOUGHTS

Let's look in more depth at how the energy of our thoughts works, and focus on how to be more aware of our spiritual energy to learn to channel this inner strength in a way that is of benefit to both ourselves and others.

If we are stuck or trapped in our own thoughts we will not have control over them. When we observe them, we separate ourselves from them and we provide a space, and this is how we can control them and channel them in the direction we wish. In order to have control over something we must look at it from a certain distance, like an impartial observer, so that we can contemplate ourselves with greater clarity. This practice helps us to realise the influences, both positive and negative, that there are in our life.

Observing our thoughts is the first step in understanding them and, in the last analysis, taking full responsibility for them.

The Energy That Motivates Us
Humans live and express themselves by means of four energy forms:

Physical:
You breathe, eat and drink, and through this process you exchange atoms and molecules with the external environment and the inner environment of your body. A part of this energy will be used for growth and another part for physical movement.

Mental:
The energy and power of thought. This energy has a big influence

over the origin of many illnesses, so much so that it has been estimated that as many as 85% of them have a psychosomatic origin. Your thoughts are also the seeds of your feelings, your mood and your attitudes. We will go on to describe the different effects of thought at a material, emotional, physiological and spiritual level.

Emotional:

This is related with how you feel, moody or happy, anxious or nervous. If your feelings are negative, it will end up affecting your body. Feelings of irritability, anxiety or tension can cause stomach ulcers. Along the same lines, with positive feelings you will be able to overcome any illness much more easily.

Spiritual:

This is related to our innate qualities and values. It is the energy of the spirit. Our perspective of the world will depend on the state of our conscience. Spiritual energy guides and provides quality to our thoughts, and that is why it is the highest in the hierarchy.

These energies form a hierarchy, in which physical energy is the lowest and spiritual energy the highest. If we are able to correctly channel the spiritual energy it will influence all the others in a positive way, beginning with our conscience, our feelings, and ending with our body.

There is a parallel between physical and spiritual energy.

Energy is neither created nor destroyed, but transformed into other energy forms.

Energy follows a direction in its constant movement.

In a spontaneous way, it tends to go from a concentrated state into a state of expansion. For example, after a while a full glass of hot water goes cold. This is a law of physics according to which all things tend to go from a high-energy state to a low-energy state.

Applying these principles to the area of our conscience, our thoughts and feelings, we can discover similarities to these laws.

When our thoughts (which are metaphysical energy) are

directed towards the outermost layers of our conscience, towards our external world (objects, possessions, people and so on), our creative capacity decreases, weakening us on entering into this expansion and not having sufficient power (concentrated energy) to take on adverse situations and circumstances that we are faced with.

In contrast, if we focus on our intrinsic, original and genuine qualities (peace, love, strength) we accumulate more energy and our inner strength can grow. This means that we are capable of creating, of having more willpower and, therefore, strengthening our self-esteem.

Positive thoughts are a high-frequency vibration that transports a great deal of concentrated energy, capable of influencing the atmosphere and the consciences of other people in a subtle way, transforming any negative vibration.

Negative thoughts are a low-frequency vibration that causes the energy to become dissipated. They weaken and block communication. They destroy harmony.

Where you focus your mind you direct your energy.

The Creative Power of Thought and Its Effects
Our mind continuously produces thoughts, which means that we are in a permanent state of creation, although we are not aware of it. Our lifestyle and our way of being are directly related to the creative power of our thought.

René Sidelsky observes the effects of thought at a material, emotional, physiological and spiritual level in his book *El poder creador de la mente* or *The Creative Power of the Mind*. These are some of these effects:

Material effects of thought
The creativity of thought is so great that the human being has invented electricity, computers, the telephone, satellites. All these things originated with a thought and are used to transmit these thoughts. Architectural works are the result of a series of thoughts

that have materialised into plans that were then built. Airplanes were created with the imagination of the human being who wanted to fly.

Emotional effects of thought
René Sidelsky tells us a classical Hindu tale as an example to illustrate the emotional effect of thought:

> "One night, after seeing a documentary on television about snakes, I got up and went for a walk in the garden with my friend. While walking, I suddenly realized, horror stricken, that I had just trodden on a curled up cobra. I froze, without breathing, petrified with fear. I thought it had bitten me and I started feeling bad. I looked more closely. My friend, surprised, showed me that it was a rolled up hosepipe. The though of 'It's a cobra' created a disturbed emotional state, a fear of dying. The effect as regards my reaction was the same as if there had been a cobra beneath my feet. On many occasions our emotional states are the result of our mental perceptions of situations and events that occur in our lives."

Physiological effect of thought
The power of thought can sometimes make a person better or ill. Many doctors accept that some illnesses are the result of mental attitudes and are caused by psychological factors (for example, stomach ulcers are the result of stress). In other words, many illnesses have a psychosomatic origin. Medicines often work through what is known as the placebo effect. They may not have a big effect physiologically, but are curative because the patient is convinced that they are effective medicines.

Spiritual effect of thought
The people who go deeply into their spiritual identity, through meditation and reflection, learn to release positive energy that manifests itself in the qualities of peace, love, purity, happiness, wisdom and serenity. The effect on oneself on freeing this spiritual

energy through these thoughts is that you reach a state of mental stability and inner strength.

In this way human beings restore all their inner potential. Your presence, wherever you may be, creates a catalysing effect on the people around you, bringing out in them the most positive human qualities. The spiritual effect of your thoughts is deeper and subtler, since you function by transforming an ordinary and limited conscience into a deep and unlimited conscience, crossing over the boundaries that human beings have created in their minds and freeing them from their inner restrictions.

When we are more aware of how we think and feel, we recognise the most positive and beautiful traits of our personality, but we are also aware of the negative habits we have created, and can appear in the form of fears, prejudices, or addictions.

The first, and one of the most important steps in transforming these negative personality traits, is to recognise them, and from there show the solid determination of wanting to transform this darker part of our being.

The Impact of Worrying

Every person has different concerns: health, the family, work, traffic, environmental pollution, the public debt, wars, the nuclear threat, climatic change... One way of seeing how positive a person you are is to examine in what you invest your thoughts, time and energy. Some of the things that concern you are out of your control, you are unable to change them, and these enter into the area of worrying. There are other things that you can do something about and these will be in your area of influence.

Example of worrying:
However much I worry about and am obsessed with unemployment and how difficult it is to find work, this is not going to help me get a good job.

Example of focusing on your area of impact:
Try to prepare myself in the best way possible. Go to a job interview full of confidence: "Although there are only two jobs for five hundred applicants, I am qualified for the job so this job will be for me". Create an image of success by focusing on specific thoughts.

Let's do something practical:

Make a list of the things that worry you most and decide if they are in your circle of influence or worry. Think about what you can really do to have an influence on each of them in an effective way.

By determining which of these two circles is the centre around which most of your time and energy revolves, you can discover a great deal about your level of positivity.

Positive people focus on the things they can do something about. If necessary, they change their attitude. They are aware that perhaps they cannot change the circumstances but they can improve their inner attitude.

This is what positive focusing is all about: being creative, thinking differently, being open to listening, being more understanding, more communicative and showing more solidarity.

Reactive people focus on the problems of the circle and on the circumstances about which they have no control. They react to the defects found in other people. From this worrying, accusations, destructive criticism, feelings of blame, a reactive language and feelings of impotence and frustration can arise. They want others or the circumstances to change first and when that happens, then they will change.

Whenever they think that the problem is on the outside, this thought is the problem. The negative energy produced as a result of this approach, combined with the lack of attention to the areas in which they could do something to improve the situation, means that the area of influence decreases in size. They give power to what is external so that it dominates them. In other words they think that change must come from "outside towards the inside"; they think that something that is outside must change before they themselves change.

Meditation helps you to work on yourself instead of worrying about the external conditions, so that you can have an influence over the conditions. This shift in attitude being part of the solution and not part of the problem.

The positive attracts the positive, whereas the negative attracts the negative. If there is hate, resentment, jealousy or vengeance in your thoughts and feelings, you will attract people in similar situations.

> This is how you think, this is your life.
> Sow a thought, harvest an action.
> Sow an action, harvest a habit.
> Sow a habit, harvest a character.
> Sow a character, harvest a destiny.

If you want to be successful when you start or create something new, sow thoughts full of determination, confidence, perseverance, enthusiasm, positivity and stability, whether you start a new day, a new job, activity or project, or a new stage in your career or your life. Creating these kinds of thoughts on beginning any activity will help you achieve success in your life easily in everything you do.

If you want to change your behavior, concentrate on the thoughts that produce it. Thoughts are like seeds: our attitudes and our actions sprout from them.

CHAPTER 3

UNDERSTANDING THE DIFFERENT THOUGHTS THAT THE MIND CREATES

To discover the art of positive thinking, it is a good idea to know and understand the kinds of thoughts that our mind can create. Four kinds of thought are usually produced in our minds. They can be categorised as positive, necessary, useless and negative. Thoughts can also be subtle or spiritual, violent or destructive. By understanding each one of them we can keep the beneficial thoughts and discard those which are useless or harmful.

Necessary Thoughts

Necessary thoughts are those relating to your daily routine, such as, "What am I going to have for supper? What time am I picking up the children from school? What is the number of my bank account? What have I got to do today?" They are also thoughts connected with your profession or job. These necessary thoughts relating to your daily life come into your mind according to your responsibilities and needs at a more physical, material and professional level.

When these thoughts are repeated over and over again, they become unnecessary or superfluous thoughts.

Unnecessary Thoughts

They are thoughts that are produced at untimely moments that fill us with worry and anxiety when they appear in our minds. They have no constructive use or are particularly negative.

Unnecessary and useless thoughts are quick, repetitive and useless thoughts that lead you nowhere. Often they refer to things from the past: "If this hadn't happened? Why did she have to say that to me?"

Too many thoughts are about things that we cannot change, or worries about the future:

"What will happen tomorrow? How will it happen? What will I do if I find myself on my own?"

"If I had been there at the time, this disaster would not have happened."

"If I had had this information at the time, I would have won the case."

"When I get the qualification, I will be more respected by my superiors."

Your ability to concentrate is weakened by useless thoughts. If you have a lot of these thoughts you use more energy and time to undertake each task. The origins of negativity also reside in them.

It is best not to pay much attention to this type of thought. A piece of practical advice is to try not to use too many conditional verb tenses, whether talking about the past or the future.

From the time that the past has already passed and the future is yet to come, these kinds of thoughts are not useful and they also weaken your inner strength and exhaust you. It is vital that we learn to avoid this pattern of thinking – in other words, learn not to create these thoughts. In this way you will be more centred and be clearer to take appropriate decisions.

Negative Thoughts
Negative thoughts harm you and are not good for you. As well as the impact they may have on others, these thoughts disturb your peace and weaken your inner strength. If these thoughts occur on a regular basis, they can cause health problems, both physical and mental. They can even become destructive.

Negative thoughts are based on rage, possessiveness and greed. They are chiefly caused by selfish and harmful reasons, without taking into account the values and inner qualities of the person.

"If he speaks to me again in that way I'll wring his neck" (rage).

"An eye for an eye, a tooth for a tooth" or "He who lives by the sword, shall die by the sword" (vengeance).

Negative thoughts also arise from unsatisfied expectations, in disagreements, in laziness, vengeance, attachment, racism, jealousy, criticism, hate and an excess of power.

"The English are more intelligent than the Irish" (racism).

"I think they should pay me more without having to do any more work to earn it" (greed).

"My boss never appreciates my work but he always values my colleagues more" (jealousy).

If your thoughts are based on these weaknesses or vices, it is as if you had poisoned your own mind and the atmosphere around you. However much you may be right, it does not matter. By thinking negatively you will always be the loser, since negative thoughts take away the respect you have for yourself and others stop respecting you. Generally speaking, people who think very negatively about others will often find themselves alone, even though they have many relationships. Other people will try to avoid someone who has angry thoughts since anger is like a fire that destroys and causes damage, and nobody wants to approach this fire.

A negative person who only sees the negative side of things causes disharmony in their immediate environment. These types of thoughts are more prevalent in people today, and are one of the causes of stress, fragmentation, aggressiveness and suffering in our current society.

At a practical level, negative thoughts make you lose energy and weaken you. They are a form of inner pollution that must be cleansed so that your mind becomes a more efficient tool.

We are quite accustomed to seeing the negativity in the world around us. Nevertheless, constantly directing our attention towards it, we have not managed to change it for the better.

In the following diagram we can see how the initial thought determines the whole process until reaching a conclusion that is totally connected to the seed that was sewn at the beginning. If we believe that we are going to fail, we will provoke a failure. If we think that we are going to succeed, we will accumulate the energy required to achieve that success.

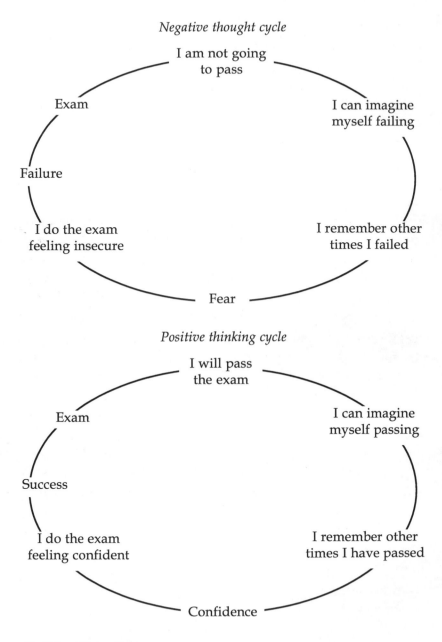

Negative thought cycle

I am not going
to pass

Exam

I can imagine
myself failing

Failure

I do the exam
feeling insecure

I remember other
times I failed

Fear

Positive thinking cycle

I will pass
the exam

Exam

I can imagine
myself passing

Success

I do the exam
feeling confident

I remember other
times I have passed

Confidence

Positive Thoughts

Positive thoughts are those that enable you to accumulate inner strength and equip you to be constructive. Positive thoughts are always beneficial in all circumstances, without trapping you in the external appearance of a situation.

Thinking positively does not mean ignoring the reality of your world and living in a fantasy or longing to be another person. For example, if you were to repeat over and over again, "I am well, I am well," when you were ill, this is not what we mean by positive thinking.

Thinking positively involves looking at problems and recognizing reality, but at the same time being able to find solutions without becoming obsessed or confused.

This often requires tolerance, patience and common sense. It is easy to be pessimistic or optimistic, but you need to be more careful and mature if you want to be a realist.

A person who thinks positively is aware of the weaknesses of others, but even then will direct their attention towards their positive tendencies.

Positive thoughts make you happy and as a result your expectations of others decrease.

This does not mean that they do not matter to you, but that you no longer demand love, respect, recognition, or even calm, from them, and it makes your relationships that much easier.

This is the best way to create long-lasting and harmonious relationships.

When you have inner happiness, you have the strength to accept other people as they are without wanting them to be different. This acceptance produces more peaceful relationships.

With the positive attitude you create, you can offer yourself to other people just the way you are, with your virtues and limitations, without pretence.

Your body also benefits greatly, since when you have a balanced, harmonious mind you are less susceptible to illnesses.

A person who has many useless thoughts will often feel very tired because they are spending their energy in creating thousands of unnecessary and inefficient thoughts.

Your mind is strengthened and healed by being nourished with positive thoughts.

A healthy mind is the basis of a balanced personality.

If your thoughts are positive, your attitude will also be positive. It is the best protection against negativity that you have within you and around you.

With a positive attitude you can keep calm when faced with difficulties and find the appropriate solution without getting yourself trapped in this difficulty.

A positive attitude is never associated with a lack of hope or confusion in the mind, and this clarity helps you to maintain your dignity and self-respect.

The way you deal with others or how you cope with situations, depends entirely on your attitude.

When you are capable of taking the right decision at the right time, you can save a lot of time and energy.

For people with a positive attitude, all obstacles will be an opportunity for improvement rather than a trigger to react negatively.

Be aware that wherever you direct your thoughts is where your energy will go.

By concentrating on the positive aspects of yourself, you are doing something constructive to bring about a change in yourself and your immediate surroundings.

This could be one of the biggest challenges of our time for which we need courage and confidence.

Positive thoughts emerge from your values and may be experienced as:

Comprehension
Confidence
Contentment
Cooperation
Enthusiasm
Generosity
Happiness
Harmony
Honesty
Hope
Love

Mercy
Peace
Respect
Solidarity
Tolerance
Trust

Let's look at some examples of positive thoughts, from the Brahma Kumaris book *Thoughts for Today*:

Happiness: "Happiness raises the spirit of whoever possesses it, and brings out a smile in others."
Peace: "Solutions to problems easily arise from a healthy mind."
Love: "Be as enthusiastic with the success of others as you are with your own."
Honesty: "If I am honest in all my actions, I will never be afraid."
Respect: "The only way of receiving respect is to give it first."
Mercy: "Do not lose hope in those that have lost hope."

Our mind produces several patterns or cycles of thought.

In all cases, the basic factor is to observe how the initial seed of thought causes a chain reaction that has a determining influence on the final outcome.

It is important to learn to transform negative thinking, to be aware of our thinking so that we do not create unnecessary thoughts, so as to be clearer and more focused so that we can we go through life making appropriate decisions.

Positive thoughts cleanse and strengthen the mind. A healthy mind is the basis of a balanced personality.

CHAPTER 4

MAKE YOUR MIND YOUR BEST FRIEND

Your best friend and worst enemy is your way of thinking.

The reason why we want to have a deeper understanding of our mind is in order to be able to understand how we create our thoughts, how they become feelings and how they are expressed in words and actions.

Our mind can be our best ally if we nourish it with positive, healthy and spiritual thoughts. It becomes our worst enemy, however, if we let ourselves produce useless, negative or violent thoughts.

The quality of this "nourishment" depends entirely on us.

Although external circumstances influence us greatly, we can turn ourselves into masters of our minds and overcome this influence. The amount of effort we make in striving to reach this state depends on the objective we have set ourselves. This raised objective depends on our understanding of the practical benefits of positive thinking. Without this basic recognition, we do not feel motivated to change what we need to in ourselves.

The mind is probably the most unknown part of human beings: it is so little-known that it is difficult for people to understand what it is, how it works and, above all, how to control it. Only when we understand how something works can we control and dominate it.

In our society, however, especially in the western world, we want to test and demonstrate everything. This attitude makes it difficult for people to understand what the mind is.

The mind is not something material that we can see, touch or measure with scientific instruments. The mind is invisible, but nevertheless its effects can be seen in our faces, in our words or our behaviour. For example, if you are feeling sad, although you can try to hide this sadness with an artificial smile, sooner or later your feelings will show through via your eyes or your words.

The mind is like the wind, it is invisible. We cannot see it but we can feel its effects. It is like the foundations of a house: we cannot see them but they are responsible for a building's stability.

The mind is like the roots of a tree: they are beneath the ground and we cannot see them, but even so they give the tree the strength to withstand storms.

In many aspects of life, the invisible often determines the quality of what can be seen.

You create and perceive the world around you with your thoughts and feelings. Your feelings and emotions, your attitude and your actions are determined by your thoughts. This process often occurs quickly and you are not usually aware of it happening. Since this process is regularly repeated, a series of habits is easily created.

The effort is in slowing down this process in the mind, as if you were slowing down an emotion on the television on a slow motion camera.

You can use meditation on the screen of your conscience as a way of slowing down this whole process and make yourself aware of what you are feeling and thinking, what you are doing and being aware of the result you obtain.

The Mind

The mind is a faculty of our soul, our being, the main function of which is to produce thoughts. The thoughts we create are energy. In one day we produce on average thirty-thousand thoughts. How much energy does this represent? What do we do with it?

The mind works constantly, even when we are sleeping. We cannot separate ourselves from it, it is our inseparable companion.

If you study your mind you will see that, as well as thinking, it imagines, remembers, dreams, associates, desires and even produces your feelings.

If you think about something that made you unhappy ten years ago, you will feel that unhappiness again, perhaps even more deeply than before. If you think of something that made you happy, you will also feel that happiness when you repeat the event in your mind.

If you create positive thoughts about yourself, you will feel good and your self-esteem will be strengthened, and if you create negative thoughts, you will feel depressed, with low self-esteem.

The mind opens up the way to the self.

By creating the right type of thoughts you can open up your inner potential again, and rediscover that as people we are full of positive qualities.

This will also help you to renew the vision you have of yourself.

How Does The Mind Work

We can compare the mind with a screen, where thoughts, images, feelings and associations are constantly appearing. Thoughts manifest themselves in the mind in the same way as images on a film are projected onto the cinema screen.

The mind often interprets negation as affirmation. Therefore, when we tell you not to think about something, it is as if we were saying, "Think about this" and these thoughts are produced with even more force in the mind. Therefore transforming negative habits and personality traits becomes a struggle. The most effective way of fighting is to ignore these unwanted thoughts, but we should then immediately focus our mind in another direction, thinking about something positive. In this way we learn how to develop our creativity, filling our mind with positive thoughts. Thus useless or negative thoughts have no space to grow in our mind. Thinking positively is not a battle against negativity but, with the understanding and wisdom that we develop in our intellect, we transform the negative into positive.

A Buddhist tale shows us how the mind works:

One day a monk who meditates went to see his master and asked him to give him some guidelines for his meditation during a period of isolation of three days. The master told him: "I allow you to think about whatever you want except for monkeys, you must promise not to think about monkeys at any time."

The disciple left a little surprised, thinking that it would not be that difficult not to think about monkeys for three days. On returning from his isolation and meeting up again with his master, he asked him: "How was the isolation? "Master," he replied, "I cannot understand what happened, because for three days all I could think about was monkeys."

It is of no use to struggle against, repress or negate negativity: it will come back time and again.

A simple solution is to replace it with something new, creating something better.

We can compare the mind with a naughty child who is playing with a dangerous object: if you take it away from them they will start crying and kick up a fuss until they get it back again. Perhaps a more effective method would be to offer them something that would be of more interest to them and in this way, by having a new inoffensive toy in their hands, they will leave the dangerous object alone.

Giving the mind creative, interesting and positive thoughts, we overcome the tendency to think negatively more easily.

Where Are Thoughts Produced?
You Are What You Think – So What Do You Think?

The saying goes, *You are what you think,* and the question is, *What do you think?*

A large percentage of your thoughts are determined by what you perceive through your senses. Everything you see, listen to, smell or feel causes some reaction or other in your mind. See how your senses are connected to your mind. Any negative thing that they pick up or produce will disturb the mechanisms of your mind. If you want to have spiritual peace, then use your eyes, ears and mouth with caution.

Other thoughts arise from the impressions that have been recorded in your subconscious, and they may be positive or negative. The negative ones are often due to deep marks and/or habits caused by past events, to everything that is deeply established and settled in your inner self.

The sight and hearing senses are those used most in human beings, with as much as 80 per cent of the information we receive being processed through these two senses.

We should always be on the alert to ensure that nothing "dirty" enters these two doors that might contaminate our mind.

From the Orient comes the saying, "The mind is a sacred temple into which only the clean and positive should be admitted". That is why we need a guardian to ensure that nothing negative penetrates into the temple of our mind.

This guardian is our intellect, the part of our conscience that contains the wisdom and capacity to discern between right and wrong, beneficial and harmful, truth and falsehood.

To sum up, thoughts are created from the information that comes from the outside and which enters our mind via the organs of the senses, or they emerge from the storehouse of information (experiences) that is in our memory.

We could compare this memory with the hard disk of a computer: each thought, word or action is stored in this memory bank. We could also call it our subconscious, identity, personality and/or character.

Observing the mind, we can be aware of the thought patterns that originate in our subconscious.

It is important to understand that "you" are separated from "your" thoughts.

You are not your thoughts, but your thoughts are created by you. With this in mind, you can be the observer of your thoughts and maintain the appropriate relationship with them.

With regular practice of meditation you will be able to choose at any time which thoughts you are going to focus your attention

and energy on and which ones you wish to disregard.

Perception

The factors that contribute to creating perception are the memory and reminiscences, experiences, beliefs, values, people, places, situations and time. Out of all these factors there are two which are chiefly responsible for creating our perception: our beliefs and our experiences.

For example, if someone believes that the English are better than the Irish, and they have this ingrained in their subconscious, this thought will form part of their perception of the world. Perhaps not only part of their perception: they may even identify fully with this belief. In other words, the thought becomes a belief and finally one identifies with the belief.

The first thing you should do is have a clearer perception of yourself. You should develop the perception of who you really are and what your true identity is. This does not refer to the image you see every day in the mirror.

Your external appearance, your physical beauty and your age should not be the basis for your self-esteem. They are merely the basis for comparing yourself with others. What is the image of your inner self? How do you see yourself?

You must know the conscience of the self, the conscience of oneself, which means: Who am I? You may live with others or alone, have a family, run a business or have another job, which you undertake with your responsibilities.

What is your conscience, however, while you are doing these tasks?

The effort made means finally knowing how to have a clear perception of yourself.

We have been brought up and conditioned to have a perception of everything that is external: perception of time, of other people, of other countries, of television programmes, of what our neighbours are doing, and so on.

However, the last thing we have a perception of is ourselves. We thus lose the link with our own happiness and our own peace.

When we re-establish the perception of our true identity, we are capable of recognising all the false beliefs about ourselves that have taken root in our inner selves. When we discover these beliefs we are capable of recognising the parts we have to change.

There are four main criteria that may influence how our perception of reality is distorted or altered. These are:

• *Mental positioning*
It is the perspective from which we see situations, and may be positive or negative.

For example, we are really excited about owning a vehicle, but after buying it we start worrying about where to park it, if it will be stolen or scratched. Another example is that of the employee who has always dreamt of being promoted at work and, when they get it, start to fear losing it.

According to our mental positioning we are frightened or we feel secure. A correct mental positioning broadens our conscience and improves our lives and relationships.

To live in the present in a relaxed way and planning the future with an open and optimistic view, we should be able to free ourselves from preconceived ideas and the influences that dominate us. To do this, the best mental position is that of being an impartial observer. In this way we can observe, recognise and transform those thoughts or attitudes that cause pain, anxiety and stress.

• *Mental limits*
Albert Einstein said that, "the important problems we face cannot be solved at the same level of thought we are in when we create them".

Mental limits are those which we have imposed on our mind. They may be limits of time, space resources or people. We create these limits ourselves or they can come as a result of our education, the family environment and the society in which we live.

For example, at work a mental limit is always thinking in the same way. So we always take the same decisions and get the same results. Experience itself may also generate mental limits.

You think you know how to do certain things and these convictions act as mental limits. The greater the mental limitation, the greater will be resistance to change.

Due to the mental limits, we usually have a series of readily prepared responses. They are excuses and justifications that provide us with poor results. We are always trying to solve problems using the same formula and this often causes stress because we cannot find the answer.

The main mental limits are related to identity. We create a very narrow and limited image of ourselves. "I am a man", "I am a woman", "I am Spanish or Mexican", "I'm young", or "I'm old", "I am white or black". The image we have of ourselves may be limited, because we do not have sufficient knowledge of our own resources, virtues, values, and identity.

A deep investigation into our inner selves will help us to change the image we have of ourselves.

Trapped by these mental limits, human beings in general only use 10 per cent of their inner potential, and the other 90 per cent is available but is not used due to oversight or the lack of awareness that they have it.

Meditating helps us to cross these mental limits. Meditation takes us to a higher dimension over our identity that releases us from these limits.

Throughout our lives, and especially during our childhood, many impressions are formed about ourselves, since at the very beginning of our lives we do not know who we are or who we should be, until we learn it from those around us, who are older, and who know more things and who presumably love us.

One of the biggest mistakes we can make in our lives is to refer only to the opinions of others to work out who we really are.

When a parent or a teacher tells a child, "You are very naughty", "You are ignorant", or "You are lazy", this child is creating negative and false images. It is quite possible that the child has said or done something wrong, but this does not mean that because of this they are bad. It was their behaviour that was bad. It is important to establish the difference between, "You are a bad child", and "It is bad to shoot across a red traffic light".

Due to the fact that many people confuse behaviour with the person, negative beliefs are created that are not based on what is true and genuine, and these beliefs may be dragged along throughout the person's life.

• *Associated memories*
In order to cross the mental limits we must work on the associated memories which create many limits in us. We always develop the habit of doing the same thing in the same space.

We have many associated memories: in fact, all addictions are associated memories. For example, the tobacco addict associates many moments during the day to tobacco (after lunch, when seeing someone else smoking, coming out of work, coming out of the cinema, in the bar with friends). Another example is when we have listened to a song over and over again. If after a few years we hear it again, not only do the words and tune emerge, but also the memories associated with the song.

Human beings are creatures of habit, and if familiar habits are broken and not replaced with others, then it may cause anxiety and stress.

In our relationships, associated memories create barriers when we relate to others, since the memories we associate with certain people and situations means that we nearly always see them in a specific way and do not give them the chance to change and improve. This limited and unrenovated vision that we sometimes have of others leads us to incomprehension when communicating.

• *Prejudices or suppositions*
They are images created in advance in our intellect and which work in an unconscious way, just like associated memories. By assuming, guessing or imagining, we create a series of suppositions that influences our perception and stops us from recognising the reality. For example, we overhear our name being mentioned and we think that people are speaking badly of us.

If we learn to rid ourselves of a whole series of preconceptions and prejudices that affect our communication and relationships, we will save ourselves a lot of time of tensions and misunderstandings.

The best way of eliminating these preconceptions is through open, concise and precise communication in order to clear up any misunderstanding.

From these four aspects, we can conclude that the way in which we analyse the world around us is very narrow. The perception we have of reality is limited. We must broaden our comprehension of how energies and how the creation of reality in the world work.

With a change in our conscience and in the way we see ourselves and the world around us our horizons are broadened.

The Functioning of the Conscience of the Self: Mind, Intellect and Subconscious

The physical body has a series of organs (heart, lungs, brain, and so on) and each plays a specific role in your state of health. Every human being also has some organs or faculties of the self: the mind, intellect and subconscious. These faculties can be in a better or worse state of health.

With an understanding of how they work and with meditation we can strengthen and improve the state of health and harmony of the mind, the intellect and the personality.

Conscious mind: creates ideas, creates desires, dreams, feels, remembers, imagines and thinks.

Intellect: rationalises, discerns, chooses, compares, decides, understands, analyses, willpower, beliefs, associates, evaluates and identifies.

Subconscious mind: dreams, habits and memories.

Personality: identity and character.

THINKING FACULTY
thinks, feels, imagines, forms ideas

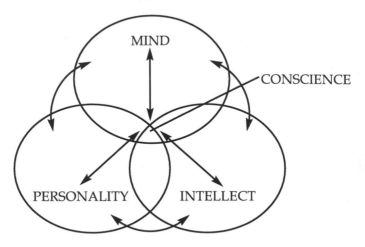

MIND

CONSCIENCE

PERSONALITY   INTELLECT

REGISTRY OF EXPERIENCES   STRENGTH OF WILL
habits, tendencies, memories,   evaluates, reasons, decides,
virtues, qualities   discerns, understands

The Intellect

The influences of strong habits or the past, deeply rooted into our conscience, are difficult to detect and therefore more difficult to check and control. However, whether the influence is external or internal (the subconscious), or both, in your inner self you have the capacity or power to filter or analyse the patterns or types of thought created, so that your words and actions can be positive and healthy, beneficial to you and others.

One of the most effective ways of changing these habits or patterns is to seek the help of a faculty that we all possess: the intellect.

The intellect holds your ability to reason. The intellect recognises thoughts as being positive, negative, useful and useless, and it serves as a handbrake or acts as a filter between the thought and the action that may arise from this thought: a filter between thinking, feeling and doing.

The intellect analyses and judges the current situation: "Do I really want this?" "Is this good for me, or am I trapped in an old thought pattern?" This is how you begin to reflect on your thoughts.

The intellect is capable of making a decision according to the information and knowledge it has stored, and suggests to the mind what is the most appropriate and beneficial. The intellect tries to convince the mind: "You know you shouldn't be doing this because it makes you dependent and makes you lose your self-esteem".

The mind does not usually accept these tips from the intellect straight away, and says, "Oh, just once more, just one cigarette, a beer, or I'll just see someone with whom I have a compulsive relationship once more; we don't live forever and you have to make the most of it".

In this way you can see how a dialogue begins between the mind (thoughts, desires) and the intellect (reason, understanding), or put in another way, between the heart and the head.

The intellect is also your voice of the conscience: all in all, you know what you should do and what you should avoid. You will have a guilty conscience if you go against what your inner voice is telling you.

A clean intellect is the filter of the mind: it separates the worthwhile thoughts from the useless ones, allowing you to put only the worthwhile ones into practice.

The Subconscious: Habits and Tendencies
During our lives we acquire diverse habits that form part of our normal life. Some of them become a part of our personality, whereas others stay dormant in our subconscious, waiting for the moment to awaken.

Of all the things we assimilate in life, the habits push us towards a pattern of routine, essential for living in society. Habits stop us from becoming nomads again or becoming totally unstable.

Some habits, however, after several years, come back to bother us. Perhaps, when you were a child, every time something bad happened, you started laughing, which at an adult age is not considered to be suitable behaviour by people who are experiencing some sort of tragedy. It is difficult to even remember when other habits began.

All inner beings have a system of natural self-control. Before doing something, the thought or feeling that motivates this action must pass through the conscience of our self to verify whether to do it or not. This does not occur with habits, since they are repeated so often, and the self-control no longer works and the person does things automatically.

It is important that now and again, when we become aware of doing something repetitively, to decide to try and avoid doing it, or at least to vary the situations when you do it, thus avoiding creating habits that in the future will become a challenge or inconvenience for oneself.

On the one hand, it is pleasant to know that all the information about our experiences, qualities, values, knowledge and beliefs has not been lost and is available to us when we need it. Nevertheless, sometimes it can become a burden. We will not always know how to recognise which "file" this comes from, since in a quick thought (which has been activated by something we will have smelled, seen, heard, tried or experienced) can lead us to a sequence of associations and often we do not recognise the cause of the feelings we are experiencing. Before we realise it, we might be trapped in an emotional whirlpool.

So how do we recognise and change? How can we ensure that these impressions stop automatically creating thought patterns and negative emotions and actions?

We must use the filter of the intellect in our self. This is also the method we must use when we want change. The power for changing, in order to be more positive and healthier, optimistic and enthusiastic, resides in oneself and not in any external influence.

The intellect, when alert, can become detached and observe how habits influence the self.

With practice, the intellect learns to filter what is correct and suitable from the incorrect and unsuitable; it tries to only place the suitable thoughts in the mind. It is important to realise that we have this inner filter that enables us to discern and to take precise and beneficial decisions.

However, even though the intellect realises what is correct and what is incorrect, often we do not have the power to put the correct into practice. This is especially true when one is stuck in certain habits or subconscious impressions, and it seems impossible to do it. For example, a person might understand perfectly that smoking a lot is very bad for their health, or that not having the self-confidence to do something they have set out to do has an influence on their state of mind. However, they have not developed the power to change such habits or thought patterns.

It is important to be aware that there are positive impressions in the self, just as there are negative ones. The positive ones can be considered as sources of energy that are eternal qualities or powers present in the inner self of every human being.

For example, peace, happiness and truth are eternal energy sources that people do not feel or express constantly. Even though sometimes the experience of peace, love or happiness is produced, it is not often constant. There is a great deal of interference from the negative impressions such as fear, doubts, jealousy, and rage. These negative impressions destroy, contaminate or block the free flow of positive and eternal energies towards the self.

The intellect must work to separate the negative and positive flows, which are often mixed, thus enabling only the positive ones to enter into the screen of our mind and translate them into feelings and actions.

How can we train the intellect to do this? How can we enable the positive flow to enter into the mind and actions? How can we check and transform the negative flows? This is what we will study in the next chapter.

CHAPTER 5

LIBERATION AND CHANGE

Freeing Yourself from Negative Influences and Habits
One of the main obstacles to positivity is the oversight that within
our inner selves there is an immense source of positive resources.
Due to this oversight, we look for happiness, love and peace in the
exterior world. In doing this, we are at the mercy of external
aspects, whether they are people, circumstances, possessions or
environments. As a result, these things or people on which we
depend to be happy. have power over us and can easily influence
us in both a negative and positive way, and we can become
dependent. When the external factors go well, we feel good. When
things are bad, we get upset and lose our inner stability.

The reason why we let ourselves be influenced is that we
identify with the people we interact with, with our possessions,
with our role or with the circumstances surrounding us. We look
for our sense of identity and value in them, but in reality, as we
will study later on, our identity has a series of bases separate from
any external aspect. Identity is how we see or experience ourselves
at any time, consciously or unconsciously. This image of oneself or
identity is the most powerful influence over our self-esteem.

The influences generate dependencies that make us lose self-
esteem:

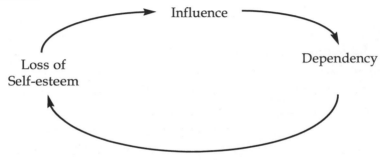

Influence

Dependency

Loss of
Self-esteem

External Aspects that Create Obstacles or Restrict our Freedom

When an external aspect influences our reactions, we are acting from the outermost level of our conscience, and we forget to use our inner values and wisdom. Examples:

Circumstances, environment

It is raining, I am sad because I cannot go on the trip (frustration).

I did not have a formal education, so I will never get a good job (resentment).

I never have time for myself, that is why I always feel unhappy (guilt).

My team has lost, I feel downcast (depression).

The media (information/news)

This government should never have been elected (criticism).

Did you hear what that criminal did to those children? (anger).

Possessions

Don't talk to me today, my new car has been scratched (anger).

My neighbour has got a new kitchen and I want one the same (jealousy/desire).

Someone has taken my books and I won't go until I find them (possessiveness).

People

That person is very intelligent, so my ideas will be of no use whatsoever (lack of confidence).

I don't like him, so I won't go to the party if he's going to be there (fear, displeasure).

I don't know what I'll do if he leaves me (dependency).

Why don't you put things where they belong! You drive me mad with your untidiness (irritation).

I know what's right, why don't you listen to me? (arrogance).

That person cannot do the job because of their appearance (contempt).

The influences of all these external aspects involve a loss of self-esteem and clarity and restrict our freedom:

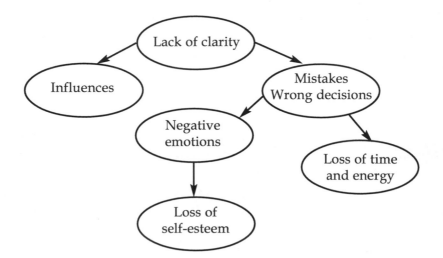

Internal Influences that Create Obstacles or Restrict our Freedom

a) Limited beliefs about ourselves and others.
b) Values with which we identify ourselves.
c) Fears.
d) Personality habits.
e) Conditionings.
f) Memories.

Freeing Yourself of the Influences

As we become more aware of the capacity we have to control our thoughts, we understand more that we can choose how we think and feel as regards the circumstances, people or possessions that may have an influence over us.

What effect does this change of perspective have? Instead of being influenced by circumstances, possessions or people, we realise that it is we ourselves who have an influence over circumstances, possessions or people, according to our positive qualities.

As a result of this new perspective, our state of mind no longer depends on what others say or do, and although we listen to them and accept their advice, in the end it is we who decide and create our mental attitude. In this way we understand that by respecting, we will be given respect; by trusting in ourselves, we will be trusted by others.

Freedom: Exercising the Power of Choice

Throughout the history of the different cultures and civilisations, freedom has been one of the values that human beings have most strived to achieve, and that yearning has been the cause of wars, revolutions and rebellions against oppression and injustice. There are freedoms such as the freedom of expression, or of beliefs, or the freedom that the nation's laws give us.

Although we have advanced a great deal in terms of these freedoms, it may be that we sometimes feel tied down to other inner conditionings, due to the influences that come from different habits we have created throughout our lives. It may even have reached a situation where these habits have resulted in a type of slavery or addiction at an emotional and mental level.

For this reason we should also appreciate that equally as important is the freedom to be able to think, experiment with and express our thoughts and feelings, without being conditioned by external factors or negative tendencies of our personalities.

Where there is conscience there is choice.

Habits

We do not take long to create a habit. We just need to think about something a few times and put it into practice and this almost becomes something that is automatic.

The thought that preceded the first action was still conscious, but the more we repeat the action the less conscious we are of the thought that created it. The time comes when we don't know why we are doing whatever we are doing: it has become a habit. We are not constantly aware of this information, but when an event or a person arouses certain feelings, emotions or desires, this reminds us of these past experiences.

A deeply-rooted habit in human nature is to project our world of thoughts and feelings onto others, and the reflection of all this comes back to us like a boomerang. We recognise ourselves in others and absorb what we see in them. This is called projection and reflection.

Many of the things we see in others are a projection and a reflection of our personality.

The way we convince ourselves of this affirmation is to look for it in our own lives. What is it that we think about gor see in others? What does it tell us about ourselves?

The Origin of Addictions: How to Overcome them

In today's society, above all in the big cities, the number of addictions and addicts is growing fast. It seems that today human beings can become addicts of almost anything: credit cards, eating, drinking, sweets, smoking, sex, relationships, television, the Internet and computer games, football, earning money, spending money, power, work, arguing, war.

In some ways, this shows the presence of an inner void that people try to fill with external things. While a person becomes an addict to any of the above aspects, their willpower is gradually weakened. And if one does not realise what is happening or does not put a stop to it, it is possible to fall into a spiralling series of automatic and compulsive actions that gradually limits our freedom to decide what we want to do with our lives, causing a loss of self-esteem and a state of depression, anxiety and dependency.

The origin of many addictions is due to a desperate need to solve a problem or a spiritual need (which may be a lack of respect, love, peace, attention, consideration) of a materialist form.

Here are a few examples:

In a cigarette: one looks for peace, calm and relaxation.
In alcohol: one looks for confidence, determination and security.

In sugar and chocolate: one looks for love, sweetness and tenderness.

In coffee and tea: one looks for energy and inner strength.

In order to change an addiction, we need to work out what need lies behind this addiction. What is the spiritual desire that we are trying to satisfy?

If we smoke for relaxation (by smoking we breathe deeply and this relaxes us), perhaps what we really need is peace of mind. Any doctor will tell you that mental peace cannot be found in a cigarette. On the contrary, instead of calming your stress, it makes you more irritable and nervous, especially when going through withdrawal symptoms.

We can learn to find relaxation and peace through meditation and will not have the need to smoke. The same applies to all the other qualities that we need to experience in our lives so that we feel satisfied and happy: it is in our inner self where we can turn to discover what we need.

Although our mind often asks for visible and material things, its needs are deeper and nothing superficial or ephemeral can satisfy it. Meditation leads us to what is genuine and eternal.

Creating Positive Habits
Some habits do not upset us, but others can cause irritation, frustration and desperation. We want to rid ourselves of them: but how?

When we look at the diagram of the creation and fulfilment of thoughts on page 20, it looks like a closed system: the thoughts lead to actions, the actions create a series of impressions, and these impressions are responsible for other thoughts, which leads us to another action.

If we want to change a habit, then where do we start? In other words, where do we change the system?

First of all, we can try changing our actions: for example, stop smoking. In many cases, however, these changes are not usually very deep-rooted and for this reason they do not last.

It may be that we have changed our behaviour, but we have not understood why we wanted to do it, and due to this superficial understanding, it is quite possible that one day we will go back to this old habit. Our motivation and determination was just not strong enough.

We can try changing this system in our subconscious. Nevertheless, by analysing what is recorded in our subconscious through different therapies, the results are not altogether satisfactory. There is always some traumatic event, or painful experience behind a fear. And although we can see and recognise our fears and anxieties, if we do not replace them with something better, with a more beneficial and healthier alternative, very often we will feel tempted to cling on to these old systems, even though they do not work and they make us unhappy. To eliminate certain things we have recorded in our subconscious, meditation and silence are the most effect non-violent methods.

Another method is to try and change our beliefs with positive affirmations that strengthen our willpower, and thus introduce a new habit to replace the old one. It is vital not to repeat this affirmation mechanically, but to introduce it into the system of beliefs we hold, and act as if we already were what we express in this affirmation.

One of our aims is to ensure that the intellect is strong and stable enough to lead the mind with knowledge and comprehension. Our mind, which is under the influence of an old program, must be left in no doubt that "I", the original personality, no longer wants to go down that old road.

When we have really taken the decision to no longer give rein to the old harmful impulses and habits, and we have the strong determination to create a new thought pattern, this will also be recorded on our memory bank.

This new register will help us to avoid taking up the old habits the next time something similar happens. For a period of time the two thought patterns, the old and the new, will exist alongside each other.

What we are trying to do is create new habits based on reason, common sense and spiritual wisdom. In this way we can gradually change our character at our own free will.

This transformation is more profound and lasting, creates satisfaction and fullness, and greatly improves our self-esteem.

To achieve this long-lasting transformation, we should not repress our mind and immediately eliminate all the habits or tendencies to which the mind has become accustomed to. If we do this, the mind will begin to cry and make a fuss, and finally, the moment we lower our guard and stop paying attention, the old habits will emerge again and drag our mind towards automatic thoughts and actions so that, almost without us realising, we are once again immersed in our old way of thinking and doing.

We have an alternative: creating thoughts of a greater quality that emerge from a new conscience and a broader vision of our inner self. In this way, thanks to these positive thoughts, full of love, harmony and creativity, the mind will start to cleanse itself, and the memories of our innate qualities will be reactivated, replacing the old habits and negative tendencies in a totally natural way.

We should understand that we cannot change others or circumstances and that the first thing we must do is change ourselves and thus understand our world that much better.

Some Practical Ways of Changing Old Habits or Beliefs

- *Motivation for Change*

An important factor to start positive change in our lives is for there to be a passion, a powerful force that leads us, a final goal that keeps us motivated. For example, an athlete preparing to compete in the Olympic Games trains really hard for several years. What keeps them motivated to train each day is the goal of being able to take part and even win a medal in the Olympics and thus demonstrate their domain over their particular sport.

In life it is important to set yourself goals, to be convinced and

to have the confidence and faith that one can reach them, since in this way we will make a daily effort to achieve those goals.

- Self-Motivation
Self-motivation is the ability to produce feelings and emotions that strengthen your ideas and thoughts and thus support and strengthen the positive affirmations.

With self-motivation you can generate feelings of love, acceptance, forgiveness, comprehension, respect, security, peace, determination, flexibility, courage, bravery and self-confidence.

One factor that helps generate self-motivation is having a series of clear goals in your life: having a clearly defined sense of purpose to your existence, clarifying the values that must guide your life in order to achieve these goals and establish the steps you must take for defining them.

If, at a subconscious level, you allow a mistaken purpose to be created, or there is a lack of true purpose in your life, then you will not be motivated to know and change yourself.

Many people think that the purpose of their life is to survive and they use the language of survival in this way: *"Life is hard out there"*, *"You must get whatever you can"*.

These people are not aware that they have chosen this purpose, but subconsciously it is what they believe they are here for, and this makes them think that they must accumulate, take, create barriers to protect themselves and compete with others.

- Visualisation
Visualisation consists of creating positive images by means of the ability to imagine, and in this way reinforce the thought and strengthen your will to achieve positively what you affirm for yourself in your mind. With visualisation you manage to intensify experiences of positive affirmations and self-motivation, and also help you to specify and clarify your goals.

Some people tend to create thoughts visually and others verbally, but in both cases visualisation is a support for verbal affirmations. The basic principle of using images in our mind is to act as if the desire we have in our mind has already been achieved.

If we place images of success, health, wellbeing or inner peace in our mind, these will materialise in positive situations and experience, and this image of success will become real in our lives.

- Positive affirmations
Affirmations are promises that we make to ourselves. They are helpful for breaking negative habits or weak thoughts that have been created as a result of mistaken attitudes. Affirmations help to strengthen the mind, although to be effective there must be acceptance and understanding behind them. It is interesting to begin experimenting with them and, later on, we can begin to create variations of new affirmations, according to our individual needs.

Here are some examples:

• *"Today I will experience peace through positivity. I will see what is good in others and will not think about what is negative or harmful. I will see others in the way I would like them to see me."*

If we focus on what is good, then this will be our experience. If, however, we limit ourselves to the negative aspects, the experience will be bad. The saying goes, *"Your world is how you see it"*.

Life and relationships can become very peaceful by taking just one decision: "From now on I will not judge others". Life is also easier when we stop judging others.

• *"Today I will speak peacefully and share peace with everyone around me. I must speak as softly as I can."*

To want to communicate peace through our words is a very high-aiming goal. It means trying to speak using good manners, which means speaking with considered thought and kindness.

In practice, this also helps us to speak less and more slowly. People who speak less are listened to the most. In essence, the aim is to concentrate on quality and avoid quantity.

> • *"Today I will make the past the past and look towards the future with a new vision."*

The past contains good and bad experiences. Nevertheless, it seems that human nature always brings out the negative. The effect is that our attitude towards the future is contaminated. In other words, future possibilities are limited or annulled due to what we have accumulated in the past. Another serious effect that recalling the past can have is the pain that it may cause our self-esteem. Recalling mistakes, moments of failure, either in relationships or in projects, is harmful to our attitude to oneself.

An effective method of freeing ourselves of the past is to take out the best of ourselves. When one can recognise a benefit in what has happened, it is easier to eliminate any feeling of resentment or bitterness.

> • *"Today I will not react angrily. I will stay calm and in peace and will not sacrifice this for anyone or any situation. I must not allow anything or anyone rob me of my peace."*

For the affirmation to be effective, we must repeat it to ourselves often, so that it becomes recorded in our subconscious. It is also important to proclaim the affirmations with feeling, believing in them and not in a monotonous and impersonal voice. As a minimum, you should repeat each affirmation five times a day.

If we listen to something repeatedly, we begin to believe in it.

In reality, this is the origin of the majority of our beliefs, hearing someone tell us over and over again when we were children. Advertising uses this technique constantly. They create a phrase, a slogan, and repeat it over and over again in the media until, finally, people believe it.

To be able to control your life, first you must know and dominate your beliefs. One way of doing this is through

affirmations.

- Conscious Disassociation
A useful method for transforming habits is that of conscious disassociation. This involves avoiding the situations that give rise to the habit occurring automatically. For example, if you often smoke after a coffee, you have to make sure there is no coffee. By breaking your habit, you will be less likely to have a craving to smoke. Instead of your habitual coffee, you can create a new pattern and have a cup of herbal tea and sit down to think or read, instead of smoking.

- Meditation
Meditation is an efficient method for transforming habits. See Chapter 9, Meditation, the Power of Concentrated Thought.

- Exercises of Silence
Exercises of silence help you concentrate your mind and intellect, and go within yourself to recover the positive and eternal energies.

With the appropriate concentration of the mind and intellect towards your constructive inner forces of peace, love and happiness, you can strengthen yourself.

Being strong means staying positive when faced with negative situations, peaceful when everything around you is chaotic: in other words, not being influenced negatively but influencing the situation with your positivity.

When you stay calm in your inner power of peace, you can transmit this peace to others and help them to calm themselves.

Always remember that **the first step towards peace is in your inner self**. When you have learned the art of filtering the negative from the positive, you will be able to give true peace and love to others.

When you begin exercises of silence, concentrate primarily on peace.

This is the basis of the practice, as when there is inner balance and harmony it is easier to build over these the other values love, happiness, truth and sincerity.

The experience of profound peace calms you, clarifies you and fills you with energy to think and act positively.

CHAPTER 6

REDISCOVERING YOUR TRUE SELF

Being Aware of Your True Self

Physical identity creates a world of limited thoughts, feelings and roles. It is disconnected from this being of inner peace and wisdom that emerges on becoming aware of our spiritual identity.

The difference between your identity, your definition of yourself and your part in the play

In one day you play many different parts in this play called life: perhaps, in the morning, you are a loving parent; later, during the day, in your job you are an executive; at midday you are student in an adult learning centre; in the afternoon, you work as a volunteer in an NGO in support of development, and in the evening, you relate to a group of friends who you have supper with.

Think for a moment how many parts you play during the day. Five, ten, or perhaps you even lose count?

Connected to the role there are many different labels that create a strong sense of identity in your personality (nationality, social status, culture, age, and so on).

Every time you play a role, you tend to identify more with it. Finally, you depend on it to create your sense of identity and your happiness. You end up thinking you are the part you play! Sometimes you can identify so much with your part that you generalise its use for inappropriate situations. For example, perhaps you are a teacher, but when you go home and are with your family you continue being a teacher and quite probably your family will not feel all that comfortable with you. Perhaps what they would like from you at that time is to behave like a good father or an attentive and affectionate husband.

The fact is, you are often changing over parts and, despite this, you still exist. Therefore you are not the part you are playing at any given moment. Through the part you play, you express who you are. Your beliefs, attitudes and thoughts are shown through these parts.

Our true identity is spiritual and we can call it our conscience, spirit or soul. We have a body which we live in and give life to. Our identity is expressed through our body. We play many parts with it on the stage of life, in the world, just like an actor plays different parts in the theatre.

Our theatre is life and there are many scenes in it which include: the kitchen at home, the office at work, the car, the shop, the committee room, and so on. Each scene requires a suitable part.

Tension and stress arise when you play the wrong part for a specific scene, or when you think you are the part itself: in other words, when you identify with it.

To preserve your own awareness as a spiritual being while playing your part in the material world requires a great deal of detachment.

The following diagram illustrates the process that connects the state of your conscience with the result of the actions you take.

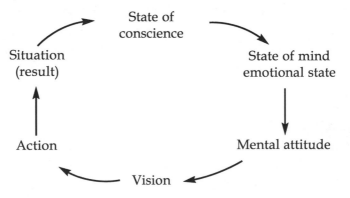

Your sense of identity will also determine your scale of values. What is the Connection between Your Values and the Different Labels You

Base Your Identity on?

If your influences are external, then your values will be more material: you will seek your happiness more in having or doing rather than in being. In contrast, a sense of identity that is based on knowing yourself and in valuing your inner qualities and virtues will mean that your values are more spiritual. The identity conditions which things you give more value to in life.

Identity		Values
Based on the profession	→	*Position / Power / Prestige / Money*
Based on religion	→	*Power / Rituals / Principles / Philosophy*
Based on nationality	→	*Prestige / Power / Money*
Based on the inner self	→	*Peace / Love / Wisdom*

In order to understand some of your fears, try to think of the six things you fear losing the most.

When they become your values, which often occurs with these identities, different forms of mental and emotional fear emerge which manifest themselves in the form of stress or anxiety.

The most powerful influences on our thoughts and emotions at any time are our sense of self-identity, our self-image and our values, which, in turn, create our perception of the world.

Perhaps what you value most in life is friendship; you value greatly a particular person and you are concerned for them. One day, however, while driving, this person accidentally hits your car. Where do your thoughts go at that very moment? "Look at the knock you've given my car? That's going to cost me a fortune! I'm going to be late for my appointment now!" or "Are you OK?"

The truth is that perhaps in a moment of pressure you value more your car, your appointment or your insurance, before valuing yourself and the other person. In contrast, at the beginning what you valued the most was your friendship with this person.

Your true values are revealed in actions and situations when you feel pressure and stress. When you defend these labels your values are automatically revealed.

The following diagram shows the different "extensions" of the self, the parts, beliefs and definitions of oneself:

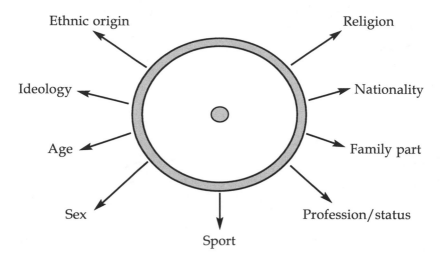

Which of the abovementioned labels is your true self? Who are you?

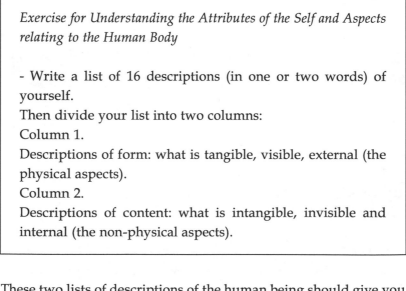

Exercise for Understanding the Attributes of the Self and Aspects relating to the Human Body

- Write a list of 16 descriptions (in one or two words) of yourself.
Then divide your list into two columns:
Column 1.
Descriptions of form: what is tangible, visible, external (the physical aspects).
Column 2.
Descriptions of content: what is intangible, invisible and internal (the non-physical aspects).

These two lists of descriptions of the human being should give you a clear idea of the difference between "the human" and "the being", the body and the conscience, the form and the content.

The mistake we often make is to identify ourselves only with the form of our body and, therefore, with the labels we give it, forgetting our true selves, which is the inner consciousness we possess.

The difference between you and your body, as a conscious being and different from the body, can be easily illustrated in the fact that your body cannot be in any other place than the room in which you find yourself.

Whereas your mind can move immediately to the past or travel towards the future while you are sitting there.

The identity of the self can be defined as a point of conscious energy that contains the faculties of the mind, the intellect and the impressions recorded in the memory that form the personality. (See the diagram on page 34.)

The labels we use to define the identity are in reality a mere description of the parts you have to play each day.

To know yourself better, you can reflect on and answer these questions:

---

a) What parts do you have to play each day?

b) What are your values in these parts and the things to which you pay most attention?

c) In what part do you feel most easily threatened?

d) Do you resist challenges and change?

Learning the Art of Letting Go and Not Identifying with the Role
The value of not identifying with the different parts you play is that you can remain in a state of positivity and self-respect when you are receiving a negative response as a result of playing your part, or when there is some kind of negative burden imposed from the outside, whether towards your part or any other aspect of your

identity. It also enables you to easily change between the different parts you play, not identifying with any of them.

By not identifying with your parts and labels, you are free to create an inner space from which your own qualities emerge, and thus you can learn to discover the appropriate aptitudes to use to play your different parts.

Seven Secrets for Meditating and Accepting the Game, the Role and the Part

1) Accept that you are something more than this body: a spiritual being, a soul. Learn to meditate in order to transcend the material form of your body and experience the lightness of your being.
2) Do not identify with a part: you are not what you do.
3) Practice being conscious of yourself and of the context in which you find yourself at any given moment. In this way you will be able to play the correct part corresponding to the scene.
4) Observe how others represent their parts, but only to learn from them, never to compare yourself with others.
5) Let others play their parts however they want. Do not try to write their script for them.
6) Always define your personality in positive terms, even though you have problems. In doing so, you will see the liberating result.
7) Understand and appreciate the unique part that you play in the stage of life.

Rediscovering Your True Self

Many people today do not have a clear sense of identity. In fact, when you ask people about the image they have of themselves, it is usually negative, and they see their weaknesses and mistakes more easily than their qualities and achievements. This negative image of oneself leads us to an identity crisis. A negative image accumulates feelings of dissatisfaction with oneself. Then our lifestyle is affected by the need for recognition and approval, by the need to justify ourselves, of obtaining material achievements and success.

Experience your True Self:
Sit back and observe yourself. What is the image you have of yourself? How do you see yourself? Who are you really? What is there left when you have removed all the labels? Are you thoughts, feelings, free will, energy, ideas, being, conscience, intellect, life? What do the majority have in common? They are internal, intangible and invisible: they are non-physical aspects. The true self is intangible and invisible.

Exercise: Your Ideal Self
Make a list of which qualities you think your ideal self should have, the self you deeply yearn to be and experience in your life.
The list should include qualities such as: happy, determined, brave, compassionate, free, loving, among others.

Exercise: Acquired and Innate Qualities
Reflect on which qualities a good professional needs today (a director, for example: efficiency, responsibility, focus, precision, determination.).
Then, leaving aside the professional aspect, explore your innate qualities. Reflect on your inner and spiritual values. Which values make you happy? Look deep into your inner self. Take some time in this reflection and note down three of these essential values in your life.

What conclusion have you come to?
You are these values.

CHAPTER 7

QUALITIES, VALUES AND VIRTUES

All human beings have original qualities that are values which define our human and spiritual nature. The original qualities of each person are similar. The only difference is to be found in the intensity with which they are expressed.

There are six intrinsic qualities in human nature: **peace, love, purity, happiness, power, truth.**

They are essential and universal values that create a common link and affinity between all human beings. These qualities, that we all possess, are expressed in our life, relationships and activity in the form of virtues.

Each of us expresses our virtues in an individual and unique way. Any virtue that we express in our life and day-to-day interactions is not usually a unique quality; normally these virtues are a variety of qualities that work together and express themselves. If we blend some primary colours, we get a wide range of colours. While we are expressing these original qualities in action, they mix together and become virtues.

For example, patience is not an original quality of the self, but it is an important virtue, necessary for keeping calm in today's world. **Patience possesses a little of the quality of love, wisdom and peace.** If these original qualities are missing, in the sense that we have lost contact with them, then impatience and irritability will arise.

The virtue of tolerance requires authenticity, acceptance and also inner strength, love and peace.

Principles are inherent values in our personality which we cannot transgress. They are fundamental values by which we live. These values are internal, intangible and invisible. Where are they, then?

This is the paradox of being human: we spend our lives in search of pleasures in food, power or position, because we think that on achieving them or having them, we will be happier, more peaceful and more secure.

Where are these values found, then? In our inner selves. When we are given a present, where is the love? In the packet? In the gift? Or in the fact that they have thought of us?

From the moment we are born, we are subject to a great many influences from our family, society, religion, education, the media, culture, social class and ethnic background, that affect our basic values and often restrict our ability to express them. This is due to the fact that today many of these influences are tinged with negativity. The values acquired are the result of external influences, whether good or bad, over our basic and innate values.

The Balance Between Masculine and Feminine Qualities

These are some examples of masculine and feminine qualities:

Masculine	Feminine
Logical	Intuitive
Verbal	Silent
Brave	Affectionate
Enthusiastic	Serene
Enterprising	Patient
Flexible	Tolerant
Creative	Inspiring
Responsible	Optimistic
Self-confident	Resistant
Jovial	Mature
Detached	Sweet

Opening up to the spiritual consciousness makes the masculine and feminine qualities emerge from our inner selves. As we become more conscious and attentive, we come across a balance between masculine and feminine qualities, achieving greater harmony in our lives and in our relationships.

When we are only aware of the physical form, a part of our being may remain hidden.

For example, if a man only identifies with his masculine form (I AM a man), his feminine part does not develop. In the same way, many women have not developed their masculine qualities due to the thought: "I AM (only) a woman".

Whether we are a man or a woman, we all have masculine and feminine qualities. In order to live a balanced and harmonious life, we need to express the two types of qualities.

Understanding the complementary nature of these qualities, irrespective of whether you are a man or a woman, allows both these qualities to emerge naturally, since they are inherent in all humans.

It all depends on our conscious state. When we are in some challenging situations we can see how the dormant part of our inner self that speaks of this complementary nature is activated.

For example in a family where the father is often absent and cannot provide his support for long periods of time, the role of the mother takes on another broader dimension. She can make the masculine qualities emerge, combining authority and bravery with her more feminine aspects.

"The world mother image is the feminine principle, which is all about virtues like mercy, love and patience. Virtues like these are exactly what the world needs most nowadays, and of course, both the feminine and masculine principles are to be found in each and every human being".[1]

If a correct consciousness exists, we can have both types of qualities in our inner selves, not only the external enthusiasm, but also the internal motivation. In this way, relationships will be fuller, since we will not have to depend on others to exist. We will be complete and not have "halves" looking for other halves.

---

[1] Dadi Janki, *Wings of Soul: Emerging Your Spiritual Identity*.

Addiction to relationships, in other words, the dependency on other people, is to a large extent due to an imbalance in our inner selves. The main reason why this happens is that we do not develop the qualities that we are missing internally and we seek the company of others who have these qualities. In some ways we can see whether we are becoming dependent. We try to compensate for our weaknesses and fill our defects by taking what we are missing from other people, thus becoming dependent on them. Without us realising, the relationship sometimes becomes like a game of cards or a business deal: "If I give you sweetness, tenderness and love, you must give me bravery, courage and enthusiasm".

Learning to Know Yourself

The more we really understand ourselves, with our defects, weaknesses, virtues and values, the better our relationships will be with others. We will understand when they have little under-standing of themselves and others.

Knowing oneself in-depth, taking into account everything described above, requires time, effort, observation and the practice of silence. In silence one can begin a conversation with oneself. In this way we can gradually discover our inner beauty and strength, and be aware of the basis of our value and dignity as human beings.

When we relearn to see ourselves with our original qualities and innate values, it is also easier to recognise these qualities in others.

Strengthening and Expressing Our Virtues

Being aware of our genuine state of the self involves recognising and feeling the full state, with all the qualities we have mentioned in the previous chapters. When we find ourselves trapped in the more external identities of name and form, the virtues remain hidden or they are used mistakenly, which means they are used for negative, selfish, destructive, violent and even war-like purposes.

When we reconnect with our original qualities, we recover the courage and confidence to be ourselves without pretending, harming or showing off.

These are the main virtues that a human being may strengthen and express:

Authenticity	*Happiness*	*Respect*
Cleanliness	*Honesty*	*Royalty*
Cooperation	*Humility*	*Satisfaction*
Courage	*Introspection*	*Serenity*
Detachment	*Kindness*	*Stability*
Flexibility	*Maturity*	*Surrender*
Lightness	*Naturalness*	*Sweetness*
Generosity	*Patience*	*Tolerance*
Gentleness	*Precision*	*Wisdom*

In as much as we express the virtues, we become familiar with them and learn to use them so that they form a natural part of our expression and day-to-day life.

This action strengthens our minds and the capacity to maintain a positive attitude towards others, whatever their behaviour.

Practicing the virtues is essential for maintaining inner stability, both mentally and emotionally. For example, if we do not put up with a situation or if we do not adapt to a sudden change in the company, this destabilises us internally and when we try to meditate in silence our mind does no concentrate, since this situation appears over and again on the screen of our mind.

Experiment with the virtues
Reflect on and write down in a notebook or on a piece of paper the strongest virtues or qualities of your personality. If you wish, you can think of them yourself and/or take them from the above list. Those which are most familiar to you are your strongest virtues. Then note down three or four virtues you would like to develop.

You can meditate about these qualities. Try to experiment with them, starting with those which are closest. It might be a good idea to look for the definition of this quality in a dictionary. Devote 15 minutes each morning to this exercise. During the day, try to be aware of each time you use this virtue you are working on. In the evening, devote another 15 minutes to meditation or reflection to look back over the day.

Try to return to the experience of the virtue and feel how you have used it.

Also look back at situations where it would have been useful to use this virtue: in other words, where it would have been necessary to use it, and visualise yourself practicing it.

CHAPTER 8

CREATING OUR OWN REALITY

The Eight Mental Laws

If we want to recover our highest, most positive state of conscience, there is a series of principles or mental laws that we need to know. Living in harmony with these principles, we will know how to get the most out of our inner resources and learn to create a present full of success and wellbeing at all levels, be they physical, mental, emotional or spiritual, for ourselves and our relationships with others. We can check their accuracy through our own observations and personal experiences.

The First Law of Cause and Effect

The law of action and reaction is a law of nature, known as Newton's Third Law. It remains the basis of classical mechanics: *For each action, there is an equal or opposite action.*

At a spiritual level, there is also an action and reaction, known in the East as the law of karma. In essence this means the results of our actions. We reap what we sow. If we sow seeds of hate (in our thoughts, feelings or attitudes), we cannot expect to receive love, respect and peace.

To imagine how the law of karma works, consider what happens when we throw a stone into a lake: it causes ripples that spread out towards the shoreline, before returning to the centre point.

Human beings constantly emit energy. We give off thoughts, emotions and feelings that transmit vibrations. There are people who tend to irradiate energy and others who tend to absorb it. The energy we give off hits other people and rebounds back to us. From this law we should understand that if people send us energy that is not very pleasant, perhaps it is because on another occasion we sent out this type of energy, although it may have taken a long time to come back to us.

If we endeavour to give off positive energy, with love and respect for others, this energy will also come back to us. Positive energy creates a higher vibration than negative energy. Irradiating positive energy produces an aura around us that protects us from negativity or from feeling hurt or humiliated. The ego makes us susceptible to criticism, lack of respect and slander. If our ego does not take over, the negativity will not touch our inner selves.

Understanding the law of action and reaction (the law of karma) requires an in-depth study of the dynamics of time, action and conscience and of how we relate to each other in life.

The Second Law of Focus and Attention
Wherever we focus our attention is where our thoughts are directed with most frequency and interest. Thus energy is produced in this direction, whether positive and beneficial energy or negative and harmful energy.

If we have a complicated mind, which thinks too much about certain things unnecessarily, our attention may be led towards the obstacles, problems, upsets and the things we worry about from a critical and negative viewpoint. By paying more attention to difficulties and problems, we feed these types of thoughts with our attention, so that we end up attracting these situations towards us. Finally, the problems and obstacles absorb us due to the amount of energy we have invested in them, turning what was perhaps a molehill into a mountain.

The situation does not necessarily change immediately on changing our attitude. With this inner change, however, we will have more energy, clarity and determination to face up to and change the situation. When we focus on seeking solutions to problems and difficulties with a positive and enthusiastic attitude, we attract positive energy towards us, and this helps us transform mountains into molehills.

If our attention is focused on people's defects and weaknesses, we transmit energy to these aspects and strengthen these weaknesses in the other person and in ourselves. If, on the other hand, our attention is directed at the positive aspects of others, we reinforce these qualities and virtues and help this person express them, which is also beneficial to us.

Our personality is made up of a series of values, beliefs and habits. If we wish to transfer our energy to new and positive aspects of ourselves, we must choose the personality traits that we want to emerge from us, focusing our attention and energy on them and, in this way, this virtue, value or quality will manifest itself in our life.

The Third Law of Self-Control
The more control we have over ourselves and our lives, the happier and freer we will feel. The less say or control we have over our lives, the unhappier and sadder we will feel.

We sometimes get angry with other people. Why does this happen? It is probably because they have not met our expectations or we were trying to control them and they have not let us. Sometimes, the simple expectation that a person should behave as we want them to is in itself an attempt to control them. When we try to control another person, we are bound to fail, feel frustrated and stressed. We end up with these attitudes because we carry inside us the belief that we can control other people. We believe that we can control time, the traffic and nature. These beliefs are deep-rooted and this is why we spend our lives trying to control what is impossible for us to do.

If we are capable of having power over ourselves, we can be more responsible for our thoughts and feelings. We have the capacity to choose how we respond to different situations and people that we come across in our lives. If we do not exercise much control over our thoughts and emotions, we easily fall into the tendency of seeing ourselves as victimised, and we blame others, making them responsible in our own minds for how we feel. When we do this, we are forgetting that we create our own thoughts. When this happens, we are handing over the control of our thoughts to those who influence, criticise, attack or slander us. We have given them the power over our inner life.

If we want to recover the control over our life, we must learn to control our thoughts and feelings and not blame anyone else for them. The more self-control we have over ourselves, the less will we want to control others and our capacity to influence other people positively will be greater.

The Fourth Law of belief

Belief may be something more internal than your subconscious. Beliefs are concepts that you consider real and true, and you do not question them, even though they have no logical explanation. If we believe in something strongly, if we think that we can achieve something, then we will. What we believe will come true.

We can classify beliefs into five groups:

Beliefs about defects and weaknesses. These beliefs produce thoughts in our consciousness like: "I am no good", "I cannot do this", "I am useless", "I won't manage to complete it".

Beliefs of survival. These beliefs produce thoughts such as: "Life is short. Get whatever you can at any cost whenever you can". Life decisions are taken based on these beliefs without taking into the account the repercussions they may have on health, relationships and the future.

Beliefs that create blocks. When we label someone, we are no longer open to try and understand them. For example: "My boss is really stupid". This type of belief blocks the flow of our positive energy and stops us from connecting openly with these people.

Beliefs that strengthen the self. For example: "I am capable", "I can do it", "There is nothing I cannot be or do if I really want to", "I will overcome the difficulties and meet the challenge".

True beliefs about ourselves. They are connected to eternal certain truths, such as: "I am a spiritual being, I am eternal. God is my spiritual father". To assure us that a belief is true, we must first believe in it. Then we check it in our consciousness and if a belief is true it will become an experience. If this does not happen, we are doing something wrong or this belief is not correct.

The Fifth Law of Correspondence
The way we organise our life is a reflection of our inner life. Whatever it is like outside, is inside. Our world is according to how we think. The way our bedroom is ordered shows us how our inner world is. If we want our relationships to improve and for there to be more stability and harmony in our external circumstances, first of all we must produce this stability and harmony in our inner selves, and from there everything else will fall into place.

The Sixth Law of Expectation
In our relationships with others, it is good to want the best: "I hope you do the best thing, I am sending you my positive energy and this is my way of encouraging you and giving you courage. However, if you don't achieve what I think you are capable of, I will not feel frustrated. I will not be dependant on you satisfying my expectations, but I will always want the best for you."

If you have faith and confidence that something will happen, it is a prophecy that must come true.

This law has its equivalent in what is called the Pygmalion effect, that the expectations we have of someone, whether negative or positive, do have an effect on the person we are relating to.

Many investigations into this question confirm the influence that the expectations of educators have, both in the performance and in the behaviour of their pupils. Everything points to the conclusion that the teacher's expectations form one of the most influential factors in the academic performance of their pupils. If a teacher expects good results from their pupils, their performance will be much closer to their real capacity than if their teacher is expecting poor results.

The Seventh Law of Attraction

Whatever your dominant thoughts are, you will attract them to your life. If you think negatively, you will attract negative things, and if you think positively, you will attract positive things.

This law also includes the aspect of vision. When you produce a very strong and clear vision in your mind of what you want to achieve in your life, and you fill it with positive mental energy, from this moment on you will attract the circumstances, people, situations and opportunities that are going to help you make this vision come true.

These are the Rules of Attraction:

Create your dream. Think about how you see yourself in the future. At this stage of your life your idea may still be tangible. You probably wanted to be a wiser and kinder person.

Identify your goals, objectives and tasks. Outline your goal; in more specific terms. Your goal could be to understand Chinese wisdom. Your objectives: to one day learn the principles of Taoism, Buddhism or Confucianism. Your task: look for a teacher and read the *Tao Te Ching*.

Turn yourself into a magnet. Have the faith that in order to achieve your goals you will attract opportunities and then recognise them. Perhaps the signs are not direct, but look for them patiently and you will not miss them when they appear.

The Eighth Law of Surrender

According to what your mind thinks consistently, you will take on the form of the object to which you have surrendered. We can see this in children, when they transfer their minds to superheroes they see on television, and then begin to behave like them.

What is the highest form to which we can surrender our self? There may be several answers to this question in our mind. Choose the truth from among them. So what is the truth? The truth may be rediscovering the part of our inner self that is unique, original and eternal, being aware once again of our true spiritual identity and thus find the answers to the questions that some of us have always asked ourselves: Who am I? What is my relationship with the Supreme Being? Where do I come from? Where am I going? What is the purpose of my existence?

CHAPTER 9

MEDITATION: THE POWER OF CONCENTRATED THOUGHT

Learning to Meditate

Just as Anthony Strano explains in his book, *The Power of Positive Thinking* meditation has three main principles or objectives:

Cleansing

Meditation is a useful method to help human beings redirect their life positively and healthily, and to achieve inner stability. The word meditation comes from the Latin *mederi*, which means "cure". Curing the inner self is not a matter of taking medicines, but it involves re-establishing the balance through knowing oneself, having the correct attitudes and making the correct use of mental and emotional energy.

In meditation, we learn to observe our inner self and recover the resources that can cleanse and harmonise us: peace, love, truth, wisdom and happiness. Through concentrated thought we learn to let these pure energies manifest themselves in our conscience and in our day-to-day actions.

Dialoguing

In Greek, the word "meditation" is translated as *dialogismos,* from which comes the English *dialogue.* Meditation is a dialogue with oneself, with the true self; a very necessary process for developing self-knowledge and accumulating inner strength.

The basis of spiritual dialogue with oneself is introspection. Introspection is the ability to examine and change oneself, as one wants to or should do. Without a consistent re-evaluation of our attitudes and thought models, negative habits easily dominate our consciousness. A healthy dialogue with our inner selves means that we interact positively with others, without being trapped or lost in ourselves. Other people and situations are our teachers. They help us to grow if we are capable of benefiting from them.

Any aspect or influence that enters our mind and intellect must be evaluated and revised. This evaluation is necessary so that no harm is caused to the inner self or others.

Introspection involves being an observer: observing and not reacting to situations or people with negative emotions such as anger, hate, fear, resentment and jealousy .

Being detached observers helps us conserve our inner energy and keeps us spiritually, mentally and emotionally healthy.

Joining: Yoga

We can take the third meaning of meditation from the Sanskrit word *yoga*. By understanding this word, we learn how to get divine cooperation, or put in another way, a certain external spiritual power that can liberate us and help us to dialogue positively with the self. The word *yoga* means "bringing together" or "joining again". Joining again with what or with whom? Firstly, with our original and eternal self: the soul, and secondly, with the eternal Supreme Source of all positive power and energy; this Source helps us to recharge ourselves with energy and to know ourselves.

At this time in the history of humanity, humans have lost the mastery and control over themselves. They do not have continual peace or a sense of purpose, happiness or fullness. The human soul needs to be recharged. Although the soul has great potential in its inner self, it needs a source of external energy for the latent powers and virtues to emerge, just as occurs with seeds in nature. The seeds of plants and trees have their own source of inner energy. However, this energy cannot be released without the actions of an external energy source, in this case the energy of the sun. Through the power of sunlight, the seeds in the earth will sprout and flourish.

The human body has its own energy, but needs external sources of energy on a daily basis: air, sunlight, water and food. Without these external sources, the human body would die.

The external source of power that helps the latent virtues emerge in the human being is not physical, since the human soul is not physical either. This source of power has traditionally been called God or the Supreme Being: in fact it has been given many names. For the moment, it is sufficient to know that this supreme power is the eternal reference point for all creation, whose task is to recharge and cleanse everything. Being eternally pure and untainted by any trait of selfishness or violence, the Supreme Being is totally benevolent, and through the eternal energies of love and truth is capable of recharging and filling the human soul with all the powers. Of course, each person chooses their own level of cleanliness, recharging or fullness. That personal choice will determine the resulting powers of love, peace, happiness and truth to be found in the individual.

The Supreme Being is like an eternal point of pure Light that resides in the world of eternal silence, beyond time and matter. Through concentrated thought we can reach this source of love and purity. When our mind is "synchronised" it takes just a second to establish communication. When we reach this place of eternal silence, the world of silent light, we focus our loving attention on the Supreme Being. If our focus is deeply concentrated we can feel how the self is filled with the purest peace and love, something we have never felt before in our lives.

This is yoga: rejoining the self with the Supreme Being and, in this union, we once again recall all the things of value that had been hidden. Yoga means remembering: remembering the original self, the original and eternal relationship with the Supreme Being and remembering, through experience, the true meaning of love, peace and happiness.

Seven Ways of Using Meditation for Personal Growth and Development

Introversion, silence and devoting time to be with oneself is essential for those who want to know themselves. Introversion does not mean lack of communication or cutting ourselves off from social relationships. Nor is it essential to sit in a quiet room with faint lights to achieve introversion.

Introversion means being able to distance oneself from all the information that reaches us through the senses (hearing, sight, smell and touch).

If we do not have this mental power and we think about every little thing we see, hear, feel or smell, we will be exhausted by the end of the day. By being connected with the inner self means that it is even possible to have an introverted attitude while we are speaking and doing things.

There are many types of meditation. Some of them have a spiritual or philosophical base, whereas others provide a basis for knowing oneself and being more aware of oneself.

There are many reasons to meditate, and the benefits it provides are very diverse: from relaxation through to cultivating inner wisdom; from concentration to enlightenment. A meditative process can be applied in many ways. Mike George describes seven ways of using meditation for personal growth and development in his book *Stress Free Life:*

Meditation as True Self Awareness
Few of us truly know who and what we are. We have learned to base our sense of identity on what we are not (position, place, possessions). Self awareness is then limited and defined by what we identify with. Meditation is the only way to see and release all our false identities, which have their roots deep inside our consciousness. BMeditation allows us to rediscover our true consciousness as beings of spirit, souls, which in turn sets us free from the insecurity which comes when we base our self identification on something outside ourselves.

Meditation as Right Thinking
The aim of meditation is not to stop thinking. Thoughts themselves can be the point of focus. Meditation allows us to control the quality and direction of our thoughts. In this way we can turn our mind away from thinking only about physical,

material things, and towards our true spiritual nature which is loveful and peaceful. Meditation helps us generate the highest quality of thinking which benefits ourselves, our relationships and our work.

Meditation as Contemplation

Everything that happens in life has some meaning and significance. Unfortunately we live so fast that we miss the deeper meaning of events and the significance of those people who pass through our lives. When we stop to 'contemplate' a certain situation or even just an object, we are using a meditative process to allow the event or object to awaken meaning and significance within our consciousness. If you reflect and contemplate on any scene at work today or on any current relationship, it will open like a flower to reveal insights and observations which can help you in such scenes and relationships in the future.

Meditation as Visualisation

We are all artists and our mind is the canvas. If we create a peaceful scene on the canvas of our mind, and meditate on that scene, holding it in our mind, investing it with depth and richness, we will begin to generate feelings of peace and contentment. At the other end of the spectrum, if we envision our goals, our preferred future achievements, then we will begin to attract towards ourselves the energies and circumstances to make it happen. Meditation helps us to concentrate and create – inner skills which many of us we have lost in our fast and frenetic cultures.

Meditation as Silence

The most powerful place within our consciousness is at the core – it is the place of silence and stillness. It is the aspect of each one of us that never changes. It is also our inner source of personal power – the power which we need to think positively and discern correctly. Meditation is our way into that inner silent space, and on the way in it allows us to see all the memories, experiences and attachments which block the way and generate inner noise. Once you arrive 'in silence', peace is present, love is discovered and a natural awareness of truth is restored.

Meditation as Communication
The context of all our lives is relationship. The currency of our relationships is our communication. At every moment we are sending messages to each other, whether we are aware of it or not. Despite the amazing toys we now use to talk to each other across the world our comunication is breaking down. We live in a globalised world, but in separatist societies. Human communication is much more than just words, and certainly more than the packets of data which we send down the line. Real communication is filled with intimacy, deep feelings and invisible messages. These messages are subtle and much deeper than words can ever convey. To commune with each other at these subtle levels is not something we learn in any academic forum. This inner sensitivity and capacity for true intimacy is an inner development which requires as much time in introspection and contemplation as it does in interaction. It is in meditation that we relearn how to cultivate, transmit and receive the kind of subtle communication which comes from our heart and soul.

Meditation as Creativity
The one capacity we all have in common is our creativity. True creativity begins within, with our self. This is not self indulgent or escapist, it is the process by which we can choose the qualities of our own character. To meditate on patience is to create patience within our self, to meditate on a generous heart is to restore generosity to our hearts. In time all those around us will benefit. This makes our personal meditation a gift to our relationships as we create and bring the best of ourselves to others.

The Value of Practice
The time we spend meditating is essential for keeping ourselves at peace, happy, stable and strong. Only by devoting some time each

day to travelling to our inner self to recharge our self, connecting with a source of spiritual power, can we stop ourselves from entering into spiritual ruin. Waiting until our battery runs flat leads to illness, emotional violence and mishaps which may be the result of this negligence. It is healthier and wiser to devote a short time a day to recharging ourselves.

In order to introduce everything that has been explained in this book into our own day-to-day lives, we must love the efforts we make and enjoy our spiritual practice. Only then will we be able to give shape to our ideas in a practical way. Otherwise it will remain just a theory.

When we Begin Meditating
The first step of meditation is to be able to undertake introspection free of fears or concessions. Through this exercise, we will cross the threshold that will lead us to the labyrinth of the unconscious, where we must learn to appreciate and love ourselves.

Find a quiet and cosy place. Relaxing music and soft lighting can help you create a suitable atmosphere.

Sit comfortably on the floor or on a chair, keeping your back straight and relaxed, not in a slouching position.

With your eyes open, choose a spot in front of you and fix your eyes on it.

Gradually stop paying attention to all the exterior distractions (objects, sounds).

Observe your breathing. Breathe deeply and relax.

Observe your own thoughts: do not judge them or allow yourself to be dominated by them, simply observe them.

Assert positive energy by the repetition of positive thoughts and images of yourself ("I am a conscious being" "I am a peaceful being").

Keep this thought on the screen of your mind and visualise yourself as a pacific, silent and calm being of peace.

Be aware of the thought, keep it in your mind and do not struggle with other thoughts that distract you. Just observe them, let them pass by and return to the thought that you have created: "I am a being of peace".

Recognise and appreciate the positive feelings that arise from this thought.

Stay conscious and stable within these thoughts and feelings for several minutes, without allowing yourself to be distracted by others.

Visualise yourself like this in your regular relationships and circumstances. For example, do not be passive or submissive, but active, positive and conscious in all your responses.

End your meditation closing your eyes for a few moments, creating complete silence in your mind.

APPENDIX

MEDITATION COMMENTARIES

These commentaries provide some guidelines for learning to relax, focusing on the inner self and meditating.

The mind tends to focus on the exterior or think about external aspects. Listening to a commentary can help guide the mind towards the interior and thus begin the meditation.

1: INNER FREEDOM

I relax.
I release tensions.
I create a space of silence.
I move towards my inner self,
letting my thoughts
gradually focus on the experience of peace.
For a few moments I reflect on all the things that affect me,
that have a negative influence on me,
the people, the situations;
everything that stops me from achieving a state of inner freedom.
Around me I visualise a luminous circle,
there is a great power of silence.
Nothing can take away my positivity,
my inner peace.
my strength and wisdom.
I can be free to think and feel what I choose.
Internally I am free.
I am not at the mercy of anyone.

2: BEING AN IMPARTIAL OBSERVER

I sit in a relaxed position,
letting all tension dissolve
I relax my shoulders and neck
and breathe deeply several times.
Now I focus all my attention inside
and observe what is happening in my mind.
I observe,
and look carefully.
I see myself in different situations,
I can identify the things that affect me most,
the dependencies on things and people
the various circumstances in which I see myself involved...
I observe how these external factors influence me and change my
state of mind.
I lack trust in some people,
but with others I can express myself freely.
There are many influences in my life.

There are the influences of these external factors...
I separate myself from them
and observe my inner qualities,
I begin to feel that peace, strength and love are part of my
original self
They are so strong that they cannot be influenced by the
changing external factors.
I create positive thoughts about myself.
I am a being independent of external influences,
and in my inner self there are many qualities.
I feel them.
I enjoy being myself in my original peaceful state.

3: INNER BEAUTY

I sit in a relaxed position
I am comfortable.

I let my body relax,
keeping my back straight, my legs supported comfortably on the
floor,
I breathe deeply...
Now I begin to carefully observe my mind.
What kinds of thoughts arise in my mind?
Are they positive, negative?
How are they moving? Slow, fast...
I carefully observe my mind
and remember that I can choose my thoughts.
Consciously, I begin to redirect my thoughts...
I create positive thoughts about myself...
I think about my good qualities,
I identify a specific quality that is special to me
and which I feel makes me a unique being.
Perhaps the quality is being tolerant, sweet, patient or affectionate.
I create a space in my inner self to discover my best quality,
and for a few moments I think about it.
In my mind I see the beauty of this quality and observe how I
feel...
I am sweet, I am kind, and as I experience these special qualities,
I begin to feel better with myself.
Now I imagine using this quality in my interactions with others.
How do I feel when I express and put this quality into practice?
Using a quality makes you grow,
at the same time the good feelings I have about myself as a
unique human being also grows.
I enjoy these feelings for a few moments
and little by little, breathing deeply,
I am aware that I am here
I express my inner beauty.

4: PEACE OF MIND

Now we can begin to experience creating positive thoughts about
ourselves
and see how long we can maintain them.
We must learn to become our own best friend.
A positive thought is imagining oneself as a being of peace.
Peace is considered as the power and original quality of human
beings.
In order to be able to concentrate,
let's imagine a point of light, a small point of energy in the
centre of the forehead.
Let's focus our attention on this point and begin to create these
thoughts:
Who am I? Who am I really?
I turn towards my inner self in order to know myself.
I am going to observe the screen of my mind for a few moments.
I become aware of the thoughts and images I see on the screen of
my mind,
but I do not let myself be influenced by them.
I simply observe them,
and I am gradually going to let them flow.
I let go of them,
I let them drift away.
I create a space between me and my thoughts,
between me and my stream of feelings.
I feel at peace and calm,
I can choose what I think.
The feeling of being able to choose makes me feel stronger.
I am strong, peaceful and calm.
I am positive energy,

I am a peaceful, calm being:
peace is harmony and balance.
I think about my good qualities
determination, generosity, happiness.

I think about all the positive things I have done today,
of all the good things I have learnt.
I appreciate the qualities and virtues of people.
Right now I return to the essence of my being,
to my original nature of peace and balance.
In silence,
for a few moments I remain in this thought of total peace.
I am peace.

5: INNER POWER

I sit down quietly,
feeling calm and relaxed,
breathing in and out deeply...
distancing my mind from all tensions and worries,
remaining free and at peace.
All those thoughts that come into my mind at the moment and
are not important,
I simply let them pass by...
I am the creator of my own thoughts.
I think about the power of motivation, the power of the will.
Originally, I was a being free to choose what I wanted,
to decide when I wanted it,
without influences...
Now, I return to that original state
to that inner source of deep peace and self-confidence,

Now there is a natural intuition and knowledge of what is right.
I realise this is what makes me free.

I feel relaxed and carefully observe my personality...
my character and the life I lead...
Am I who I want to be?
Does my character correspond to my ideals?
Do I lead the life I want to lead?

Am I independent?
The power to free myself is to be found in my inner self.
The capacity to feel like an autonomous being, with a free mind,
as peaceful as I desire,
as positive as I want it to be.
And my feelings are in harmony, free of restrictions, free of
influences.

The power of thoughts is so great,
if I think I can do something
the power will be there to do it.
If I choose to think positively, I can think positively.
If I want to relax my body, I can do it.
If I want to be emotionally free,
and still be in the world without bowing down to others, I can.

If I think about my own life and want to change something,
this is possible
if it is a conscious choice that arises from the depth of my heart,
if my intention is noble and pure,
the results will be good.
In this way, my life is much easier,
since I live from an inner intuition and clear understanding.
Free of selfish motivation,
I choose what I want for my own life.
This gives me freedom and makes me feel peaceful.

I ask myself over and over again:
Am I free? ...
Free to create the thoughts I want to create,
when I want to,
as often as I want to,
for as long as I want to.

I am the creator of my own world,
of everything I think and do.

6: THE BEING OF LIGHT

I am conscious of myself and of what is around me.
I look at my life as a detached observer.
I observe the different roles I play during the day.
I see to what point I am capable of releasing myself of the role
after I have played it and the scene has ended.
I can be myself.
I am freed from my roles.
I free myself of the consciousness of my body.
I become light,
without burdens, free of weight.
I am only pure consciousness
I am light.
I am a miniscule point of light
that radiates from the centre of my forehead.
I radiate the innate qualities of my being.
I radiate vibrations of peace,
I radiate vibrations of love.
I am peace, I am love, I am light.

7: RETURNING TO MY ESSENCE

First of all, spend a few moments to discover how you feel right
now.
You do not have to explain it to anyone nor write it down,
unless you actually want to.
Just let your thoughts, memories and feelings arise in your
consciousness,
without judging them, simply observing them.
Try to be conscious of what you are experiencing.
Firstly, be conscious of your body:
How do you feel?
Which muscles are tense?
Which part of your body feels relaxed?

Observe the rhythm of your breathing.
Be conscious of your heartbeat,
of the blood circulating around your body.
Now be aware of your feelings:
What are you feeling?
Do you perceive any negative feeling in you?
What are the highest positive feelings in you?
Be conscious of your thoughts
and observe the flow of thoughts as they appear before you:

Now imagine that before you there is a huge empty chest.
Start putting in all your material possessions:
books, furniture, shoes, clothes, jewels,
everything that belongs to you.
Make sure that your house is totally empty
and then also place it within the chest.

Now put in all the people you know :
friends, relatives, partner, work colleagues
and all the people with whom you spend some time.
Put everyone you know in the world inside the chest.
Now put away all the roles you play in life:
as family member, work partner, couple, friend
Now place all the judgements you make of yourself.
Place your emotions:
anger, happiness, excitement, boredom,
put away all your thoughts, beliefs, attitudes, opinions and
ideas.
Now place your body into the chest and see how it fits
Look closely at everything that is inside the chest: observe it.
With your eyes closed,
ask yourself who is observing the contents of the chest.
Now look for your body in the chest and place yourself inside it.
Get out of the chest and look slowly around you.
You will see the room in which you are sitting.
Sit in your chair or wherever you were sitting at the beginning of

this exercise.
Feel the pressure of the chair on your back,
be aware again of your body
and when you are ready ,open your eyes,
but stay in silence for a short while.

8: SPIRITUALITY IN PRACTICE

On the screen of your mind,
make an appraisal of what has happened throughout the week.
Think about the awareness that you have had of yourself.
Think about the actions you have taken.
Have they been based on a positive consciousness of yourself?
Can you see the intentions behind your actions?
Now, slowly and gently, I focus on my inner self.
I observe myself.
I recognise my positive qualities,
the things I value most in life.
I see my life with meaning and a purpose.
There is learning and growth.
There is inner strength.
I feel strong and secure and so can respect others.
I respect myself.
I love myself.
I love others.
I feel calm and at peace.
Free to experience my inner qualities.
And now, for a few moments, I am going to
create feelings of peace and serenity.
I am going to share thoughts and feelings of peace.

BIBLIOGRAPHY

Brahma Kumaris, *Thought for Today* (Brahma Kumaris Publications, 1989)

Carteret, Nikki de *Soul Power The transformation that happens when you know* (O Books, 2003)

Dadi Janki *Wings of Soul: Emerging Your Spiritual Identity* (Brahma Kumaris Publications, 1998)

George, Mike *In the Light of Meditation* (O Books, UK. New York, EE UU, 2004)

George, Mike, *Stress Free Life* (Brahma Kumaris Self Management Systems, 2001)

Janki, Dadi *Inside Out* (BK Publications, London, 2003)

Pemell, Judith *The Soul Illuminated* (Lothian Books, Melbourne, Australia, 2003)

Sidelsky, René *El Poder Creador de la Mente (The Creative Power of the Mind)* (Robinbook, Barcelona, Spain, 1991)

Strano, Anthony *The Power of Positive Thinking* (Brahma Kumaris, Australia, 1994)

Subirana Vilanova, Miriam *Dare to Live* (O Books, UK. New York, EE UU, 2008)

BRAHMA KUMARIS WORLD SPIRITUAL UNIVERSITY

The Brahma Kumaris World Spiritual University is an international organisation which works in all areas of society for a positive change. Created in 1937, at present it offers and participates in a wide range of educational programmes for the development of human and spiritual values. More than 9,000 meditation centres of the Brahma Kumaris Organisation in 100 countries offer courses in positive thinking, overcoming stress, self-esteem, Raja Yoga meditation and personal leadership.

For more information, visit the web page: www.bkwsu.org

INTERNATIONAL HEADQUARTERS
Post Box No 2
Mount Abu 307501, Rajasthan
India
T (+91) 2974 238261- 68
E abu@bkwsu.org

INTERNATIONAL CO-ORDINATING OFFICE
& REGIONAL OFFICE FOR EUROPE & MIDDLE EAST
Global Co-operation House
65-69 Pound Lane
London NW10 2HH
United Kingdom
T (+44) 20 8727 3350
E london@bkwsu.org

REGIONAL OFFICES

AFRICA
Brahma Kumaris Raja Yoga Centre
Global Museum, Maua Close,

Westlands, PO Box 123 - 00606
Nairobi
T (+254) 20-3743572 / 3741239
F 254-20-3743885
E nairobi@bkwsu.org

ASIA PACIFIC
78 Alt Street, Ashfield
Sydney NSW2131
Australia
T (+61) 2 9716 7066
E ashfield@au.bkwsu.org

THE AMERICAS & THE CARIBBEAN
Global Harmony House
46 S. Middle Neck Road
Great Neck, New York 11021
USA
T (+1) 516 773 0971
E newyork@bkwsu.org

RUSSIA, CIS & THE BALTIC COUNTRIES
2 Gospitalnaya Ploschad, Build. 1
Moscow 111020
Russia
T (+7) 495 263 02 47
F (+7) 495 261 32 24
E moscow@bkwsu.org

SPAIN
Main centre
Diputacio 329, Pral
Barcelona 08009
Spain
T (+34) 934 877 667
E barcelona@es.bkwsu.org

ABOUT THE AUTHORS

MIRIAM SUBIRANA VILANOVA

www.miriamsubirana.com. PhD in Fine Arts, she trained at the Faculty of Fine Arts at the University of Barcelona Spain, and at the California College of Arts and Crafts of Oakland, USA.

Miriam is an international speaker who combines leadership skills with the use of art and creative meditation techniques. As a public Speaker, Miriam has given lectures to different publics from over a thousand people to small selective groups in over 20 countries. She has motivated hundreds of people to transform their lives opening up to new possibilities that permit the realization of one's own potential.

She co-ordinates numerous programmes, projects, seminars and retreats whose objective is to help towards knowing oneself, re-finding ones identity and enjoying a fuller life.

She has shown her art work in galleries and exhibition rooms in Spain, Portugal, France, Denmark, England, New York, San Paulo, Hong Kong, amongst other cities of the world.

She has co-ordinated the creation of two spiritual art galleries in Mount Abu and Agra (India).

The Spanish publication of *Who Rules in Your Life?* has been re-edited four times in three years. Her second book, *Dare to Live* was published in Spanish in 2007 and was reedited for a second time in the same year with more than 70,000 books sold. She also publishes articles on matters of personal development and has recorded many CDs of guided meditations.

mira@miriamsubirana.com

RAMÓN RIBALTA SECANELL

A graduate in Law at the University of Barcelona, he has, since 1990, combined his profession as lawyer with the practice and teaching of Raja Yoga Meditation.

For the last 15 years has been guiding and facilitating courses and seminars in personal development and management skills of people in companies, schools and communities in many cities all over Spain. He is coordinator of the work of the Brahma Kumaris World Spiritual University in Palma de Mallorca, Spain.

ramonribalta@gmail.com

BOOKS

7 Aha's of Highly Enlightened Souls
Mike George

A very profound, self empowering book. Each page bursting with wisdom and insight. One you will need to read and reread over and over again! **Paradigm Shift**

1903816319 128pp **£5.99 $11.95**

Don't Get MAD Get Wise
Why no one ever makes you angry!
Mike George

After "The Power of Now", I thought I would never find another self-help book that was even a quarter as useful as that. I was wrong. Mike George's book on anger, like a Zen master's teaching, is simple yet profound. This isn't one of those wishy-washy books about forgiving people. It's just the opposite....a spiritually powerful little book. **Marian Van Eyk**, *Living Now Magazine*

1905047827 160pp **£7.99 $14.95**

The Four Faces of Woman
Restoring Your Authentic Power, Recovering Your Eternal Beauty
Caroline T. Ward

I've always thought of Caroline Ward as a competitor - because more people would turn up for her retreats than mine. After reading "Four Faces of Woman" I can understand why. For any woman who believes she's on a spiritual journey, and wondering where it's leading, you won't find a better route-map than this. **Paul Wilson**, best selling author, *"The Calm Series"*

9781846940866 272pp **£9.99 $19.95**

Celtic Wheel of the Year, The
Celtic and Christian Seasonal Prayers
Tess Ward

This book is highly recommended. It will make a perfect gift at any time of the year. There is no better way to conclude than by quoting the cover endorsement by Diarmuid O'Murchu MSC, "Tess Ward writes like a mystic. A gem for all seasons!' It is a gem indeed. **Revd. John Churcher**, Progressive Christian Network

1905047959 304pp **£11.99 $21.95**

Savage Breast
Tim Ward

An epic, elegant, scholarly search for the goddess, weaving together travel, Greek mythology, and personal autobiographic relationships into a remarkable exploration of the Western World's culture and sexual history. It is also entertainingly human, as we listen and learn from this accomplished person and the challenging mate he wooed. If you ever travel to Greece, take "Savage Breast" along with you. **Harold Schulman**, Professor of Gynaecology at Winthrop University Hospital, and author of *An Intimate History of the Vagina*

1905047584 400pp **£12.99 $19.95**

A Global Guide to Interfaith
Reflections From Around the World
Sandy Bharat

This amazing book gives a wonderful picture of the variety and excitement of this journey of discovery. **Rev Dr. Marcus Braybrooke**, President of the World Congress of Faiths

1905047975 336pp **£19.99 $34.95**

Everyday Buddha
Lawrence Ellyard

Whether you already have a copy of the Dhammapada or not, I recommend you get this. If you are new to Buddhism this is a great place to start. The whole feel of the book is lovely, the layout of the verses is clear and the simple illustrations are very beautiful, catching a feel for the original work. His Holiness the Dalai Lama's foreword is particularly beautiful, worth the purchase price alone. Lawrence's introduction is clear and simple and sets the context for what follows without getting bogged down in information... I congradulate all involved in this project and have put the book on my recommended list. **Nova Magazine**

1905047304 144pp **£9.99 $19.95**

Peace Prayers
From the World's Faiths
Roger Grainger

Deeply humbling. This is a precious little book for those interested in building bridges and doing something practical about peace. **Odyssey**

1905047665 144pp **£11.99 $19.95**

Shamanic Reiki
Expanded Ways of Workling with Universal Life Force Energy
Llyn Roberts and Robert Levy

The alchemy of shamanism and Reiki is nothing less than pure gold in the hands of Llyn Roberts and Robert Levy. Shamanic Reiki brings the concept of energy healing to a whole new level. More than a how-to-book, it speaks to the health of the human spirit, a journey we must all complete. **Brian Luke Seaward**, Ph.D., author of *Stand Like Mountain, Flow Like Water, Quiet Mind, Fearless Heart*

9781846940378 208pp £9.99 $19.95

The Good Remembering
A Message for our Times
Llyn Roberts

Llyn's work changed my life. "The Good Remembering" is the most important book I've ever read. **John Perkins**, *NY Times* best selling author of *"Confessions of an Economic Hit Man"*

1846940389 96pp £7.99 $16.95

The Last of the Shor Shamans
Alexander and Luba Arbachakov

The publication of Alexander and Luba Arbachakov's 2004 study of Shamanism in their own community in Siberia is an important addition to the study of the anthropology and sociology of the peoples of Russia. Joanna Dobson's excellent English translation of the Arbachakov's work brings to a wider international audience a fascinating glimpse into the rapidly disappearing traditional world of the Shor Mountain people. That the few and very elderly Shortsi Shamans were willing to share their beliefs and experiences with the Arbachakov's has enabled us all to peer into this mysterious and mystic world. **Frederick Lundahl,** retired American Diplomat and specialist on Central Asia

9781846941276 96pp **£9.99 $19.95**

Thoughtful Guide to God
Howard Jones

As thoughtful as the title claims, this is thorough, with excellent background, history and depth, and is just right for the kind of person who sees, feels and perhaps has already begun to find the fusion of consciousness that shows the way out of the confusion of our times towards a way of being that is positive, without being naive, and profoundly informative, without being pedantic. If you have a brain, heart and soul, and the interest to see where they become one, this book is a must. **Odyssey**

1905047703 400pp **£19.99 $39.95**

The Thoughtful Guide to Religion
Why it began, how it works, and where it's going
Ivor Morrish

A massive amount of material, clearly written, readable and never dry. the fruit of a lifetime's study, a splendid book. It is a major achievement to cover so much background in a volume compact enough to read on the bus. Morris is particularly good on illustrating the inter-relationships betwen religions. I found it hard to put down. **Faith and Freedom**

190504769X 384pp **£24.99 $34.95**

Life in Paradox
The Story of a Gay Catholic Priest
Paul Edward Murray

This memoir is the compelling story of an honest, sensitive priest, and the tragic tale of a hierarchy that has lost its way in its desire to control the Church rather than nurture it. No book sets out more clearly and urgently the tragedy and the prospects of the current crisis of Catholicism. **Bruce Chilton**, Bernard Iddings Bell Professor of Religion, Bard College

9781846941122 240pp **£11.99 $24.95**

Wojtyla's Women
How Women, History and Polish Traditions Shaped the Life of Pope John Paul II and Changed the Catholic Church
Ted Lipien

An important book. Few persons are as qualified as he is to enlighten readers about Pope John Paul II's Polish roots – and the impact that they had on his views on women. Lipien provides a stimulating analysis of the Pope's ideas on gender roles and how John Paul believed the Church should deal with sexual issues. This is a must-read for anyone interested in the relationship between feminism and Catholicism, a key issue of our times. **Dr. John H. Brown**, editor of *"Public Diplomacy Press Review"*

9781846941108 688pp **£14.99 $29.95**

The First English Prayer Book (Adapted for Modern Use)
The first worship edition since the original publication in 1549
Robert Van de Weyer

In 1549 Thomas Cranmer published the first Prayer Book in

English. Based on a medieval form of worship, its language is both sublime and majestic. This new edition presents Cranmer's services in a form which is practical, accessible and easy to follow.

9781846941306 160pp **£9.99 $19.95**

Who Is Right About God?
Thinking Through Christian Attitudes in a World of Many Faiths
Duncan Raynor

This book is both important and readable, because it has been forged in the daily "real time" interplay between the issues and views that it discusses, and because it is given rigour and intellectual coherence by the gifted author, who has an Oxford training in philosophy, as well as theology. **The Very Revd Robert Grimley**, Dean of Bristol Cathedral

9781846941030 144pp **£11.99 $24.95**

The Other Buddhism
Amida Comes West
Caroline Brazier

An essential book for Buddhists, for students of religion, and for therapists of all schools, and for anyone who seeks an improved ability to cope with the stresses of our everyday world. **Jim Pym**, editor of *Pure Land Notes*

978-1-84694-0 304pp **£11.99 $24.95**

The Way Things Are
A Living Approach to Buddhism
Lama Ole Nydahl

It is my wish that through this book, the seed of Buddhahood is planted in the reader's mind. By putting the teachings presented here into practice, may they accomplish the ultimate goal of Enlightenment for the benefit of all. **Trinlay Thaye Dorje,** the 17th Gyalwa Karmapa

1846940427 192pp **£9.99 $19.95**

Who Loves Dies Well
On the Brink of Buddha's Pure Land
David Brazier

Practical, moving and full of deep love for the reader, and as such is the perfect guide to newcomers and experienced Buddhists alike. **Jim Pym,** author of *You Don't Have to Sit on the Floor.*

9781846940453 256pp **£11.99 $19.95**

The House of Wisdom
Yoga of the East and West
Swami Dharmananda Saraswati and Santoshan

Swamiji has shared her wisdom with her students for many years. Now her profound and enlightening writings, and those of Santoshan, are made available to a wider audience in this excellent book. The House of Wisdom is a real treasure-house of spiritual knowledge. **Priya Shakti (Julie Friedeberger),** author of *The Healing Power of Yoga*

1846940249 224pp **£11.99 $22.95**

Back to the Truth
5000 years of Advaita
Dennis Waite

This is an extraordinary book. The scope represents a real tour de force in marshalling and laying out an encyclopaedic amount of material in way

that will appeal both to the seasoned and to the introductory reader. This book will surely be the definitive work of reference for many years to come. **Network Review**

1905047614 600pp **£24.95 $49.95**

The Bhagavad Gita
Alan Jacobs

Alan Jacobs has succeeded in revitalising the ancient text of the Bhagavad Gita into a form which reveals the full majesty of this magnificent Hindu scripture, as well as its practical message for today's seekers. His incisive philosophic commentary dusts off all the archaism of 1500 years and restores the text as a transforming instrument pointing the way to Self Realization. **Cygnus Review**

1903816513 320pp **£12.99 $19.95**

Helena's Voyage
A mystic adventure
Paul Harbridge

A beautiful little book, utterly charming in its simplicity. **Rabbi Harold Kushner,** author of *"When Bad Things Happen to Good People"*

9781846941146 48pp **£9.99 $19.95**